OUR SARAH

OUR SARAH

Made in Alaska

❧

CHUCK HEATH SR.
and CHUCK HEATH JR.

Foreword by Sarah Palin

**CENTER
STREET**

New York Boston Nashville

All photos courtesy of Chuck Heath Sr. collection.

Center Street
Hachette Book Group
237 Park Avenue
New York, NY 10017

www.CenterStreet.com

Printed in the United States of America

RRD-C

First edition: September 2012
10 9 8 7 6 5 4 3 2 1

Center Street is a division of Hachette Book Group, Inc.
The Center Street name and logo are trademarks of Hachette Book Group, Inc.

The Hachette Speakers Bureau provides a wide range of authors for
speaking events. To find out more, go to www.HachetteSpeakersBureau.com
or call (866) 376-6591.

The publisher is not responsible for websites (or their content) that are not owned
by the publisher.

Library of Congress Cataloging-in-Publication Data

Heath, Chuck, 1939–

Our Sarah : made in Alaska / Chuck Heath, Sr. and Chuck Heath, Jr. — 1st ed.

p. cm.

ISBN 978-1-4555-1628-5 (regular edition) — ISBN 978-1-4555-2258-3 (large
print edition)   1. Palin, Sarah, 1964–   2. Vice-Presidential candidates—
United States—Biography.   3. Palin, Sarah, 1964—Family.   4. Governors—
Alaska—Biography.   5. Mayors—Alaska—Wasilla—Biography.   6. Heath
family.   7. Alaska—Biography.   8. Idaho—Biography.   I. Heath, Chuck,
1962–   II. Title.

F910.7.P35H43 2012

979.8'052092—dc23

[B]

2012015933

To Sally, Abby, Heather, Molly, Kier, Teko, and Sophia.
Thanks for your patience and loving support.

Contents

Contents

FOREWORD

When we were kids, our view of life outside Alaska was shaped by the occasional television show and by the even less frequent movies. What we saw on episodes of *The Brady Bunch* pretty much defined our view of how every kid in the lower forty-eight states must have lived. As much as we enjoyed the show, we never wanted to trade places with those kids. They never had the joy of climbing to the top of Hatcher Pass and breathing in the clean mountain air, swimming in Lake Lucille with ice still clinging to the shoreline, or watching a coastal stream churn with the energy of a salmon run. We were certain those kids from "outside" (the term Alaskans use for the lower forty-eight) would never last a minute in our world. Even at a young age, our view of what mattered in life had been molded and shaped by the things we encountered on our family's trek from Idaho to the shores of Cook Inlet.

On the surface, our parents were perhaps as different from each other as night and day—Dad the tough outdoorsman, Mom the calm caregiver. Yet in many ways they were more alike than any couple I've ever known. Their consistency and temperament gave us a solid, unmovable foundation from which to grow and mature.

Always the teacher and coach, they used every incident in our lives to instill in us the values we live by today—those old-fashioned American values of courage, hard work, and fortitude in the face of difficulties. Most of all, they taught us that character matters and that love for God, for others, and for our country are priorities to live by. We learned those values from our parents as we grew up in Alaska, braving the cold for a morning moose hunt, ice-fishing on the lake near our home, and climbing the mountains in the spring to shoot ptarmigan. We also learned that no one accomplishes anything in life solely on his or her own, a point many people seem to have forgotten today.

When we were kids, Wasilla was little more than a cluster of homes. We knew almost everyone in the area. That kind of familiarity created a unique sense of community. More than once I remember our parents stopping on the road in winter to pick up someone who'd been stranded by car trouble in subzero weather. Sometimes they were friends we knew well. Other times they were people we knew only by sight. It didn't matter. We scrunched over on the car seat to give them room and off we went to help them get where they were going. Along the way we met some interesting characters and learned to love the Alaskan sense of humor—an ironic view of life that, seasoned with a healthy serving of pioneer grit, gives Alaskans the strength to persevere against seemingly insurmountable odds. They also showed us just how much true American ingenuity and entrepreneurship can accomplish.

Dad had a great sense of civic pride and taught us to love and respect our country and those who fought to keep our nation free. Mom made sure we were in church every Sunday and gave us a living example of humility, kindness, and a true servant's heart. They both were active in the community and always ready to help with fun runs, charity events, and lending a hand to those in need.

When we were in school, most of our friends came from the sports teams on which we played. For Heather, Molly, and me, that meant basketball, track and field, and cross-country. Chuck's friends were mostly from the football team. Later in life our circle of friends continued to expand in different directions as we each developed our own lives. We continue to see many of the people we knew years ago, though our lives have changed and life in the Mat-Su Valley has grown more hectic.

As they worked on this book, I'm sure my father and brother enjoyed recalling many memories from our family's journey. Dad, in particular, always relished time spent sipping coffee with old friends while swapping tales about the adventures of days gone by and making plans for the ones yet to come.

Talking about the past is relatively easy compared to the more daunting task of putting those memories on paper. Having written books of my own, I know firsthand how exhausting producing a manuscript can be. And while we may enjoy hearing stories from the past, others are sometimes more reluctant to tell them. Coaxing them to help by opening up their memories often can be a challenge of its own, especially now. Many of our friends have learned the hard way that what they say in conversation doesn't always appear in print the way they meant it, even when it's being written by a family member or a friend.

When Dad and Chuck Jr. started on this project, I was a little apprehensive about how things would turn out. Many books and articles have been written about us, and while some of them are honest, most are woefully inaccurate. I knew Dad and Chuck Jr. always had my best interests at heart; but I've spent my life in public service, and the political side of public service can be quite nasty and especially hard on family members. Consequently, I'm very protective of my immediate and extended family—five generations of good Americans who, like most people, value their privacy.

In the pages that follow, Dad and Chuck Jr. share with you their personal stories and their views of how our family braved the unknown and pushed forward against the harsh climate and terrain of Alaska. Surviving and succeeding in the Last Frontier demands an independent spirit, much like America's founders expected all citizens could and should share. Along the way, we had many life-changing experiences, made great memories, and developed some even greater friendships. I hope you'll be inspired by their stories and by the warm Alaskan spirit they reflect.

Sarah Palin
Wasilla, Alaska

AUTHORS' PREFACE AND ACKNOWLEDGMENTS

When we first considered writing a book, we wanted to provide insight into the events and relationships that made Sarah Palin the person she is today. We also thought it would be fun to share some of our family's many Alaskan adventures. As we worked through the writing process, we realized that while we were creating a book for the public, we also were preparing a family biography.

Doing that made us realize the importance of relationships—genuine relationships, not just spending time in each other's presence. Our family is blessed to have a documentable history that dates to the fourteenth century, but as we sifted through the surviving papers and memorabilia from previous generations, we realized how fleeting life really is and how quickly our personal stories fade from the memory of subsequent generations. That realization impressed upon us the importance of expressing our love for one another now, in the present, rather than waiting to reflect upon it later.

Many people have written articles and books about Sarah and our family. Countless news broadcasts have been devoted to the topic of who she is, what her family is like, and whether the stories about her and us are really true. We can't vouch for those prior reports, but we can assure you that the stories and events we've recorded in the pages of this book are as accurate as memory allows. This is our story and our explanation of who we are and how Sarah came to be the person she is now. Hopefully you will find in these pages the broader context of her life, a context missing from almost everything written about her. The glimpse you will see in this book is that of the real Sarah Palin—the Sarah we know and love, not the one created by the national media.

We were assisted in our effort by friends, coworkers, and family members who once again shared their memories. Many people encouraged us to undertake this project, but none more than Vicki Wolfe who kept saying, "You've got to write a book." Jean and Mark Tennant, retired teachers themselves, reviewed portions of the text.

Our efforts were made possible by colleagues in the publishing industry who assisted us with the writing process. Tom Winters with Winters & King, Inc., represented us to our publisher, where we found the invaluable help of our editor, Kate Hartson, and her staff. Bestselling author Joe Hilley spent many hours collecting our stories and weaving them into the cohesive account you are about to read. And our wives, Sally and Abby, proved exceedingly tolerant as we devoted ourselves to what became a yearlong project. Thank you, one and all, for your help in making this book possible.

Twenty years from now, you will be more disappointed by the things that you didn't do than by the ones you did do. So throw off your bowlines. Sail away from the safe harbor. Catch the trade winds in your sails. Explore. Dream. Discover.

—Attributed to Mark Twain

OUR SARAH

CHAPTER 1

Taking the Stage

And our Sarah—the one we'd known all our lives—
finally took the stage.
CHUCK HEATH JR.

Light from the street, unusually bright and glaring, shone overhead as our motorcade rolled off the highway and onto a broad avenue. Around us the sidewalks were lined with people, all of them staring at us, hoping for a glimpse through the tinted glass of our black SUV. Near the middle of the block, a row of television trucks was parked at the curb, their satellite antennas pointed toward some unseen link in the dark sky.

Moments later, motorcycle patrolmen whizzed past us, then came to a stop in the center of the street. The patrolmen dismounted and took up positions along our route as the lead car in our motorcade turned left and disappeared from sight. In quick succession, each of the cars ahead of us did the same as we made the corner and rolled down a concrete ramp that led beneath the Xcel Energy Center, an 18,000-seat arena. Usually home to the National Hockey League's Minnesota Wild, the night we arrived it was the site of the 2008 Republican National Convention.

As the motorcade idled to a stop near the underground entrance, security agents stepped up to our SUV and opened the doors. I climbed from the backseat, straightened my jacket, and reached back to offer my mom a hand. Then we followed our group inside. With me that evening were my parents, Chuck and Sally Heath; a few friends from my hometown of Wasilla, Alaska; and our mother's sisters, Kate and Colleen, who had flown in from their homes near Richland, Washington.

Just beyond the building entryway, we were met by a campaign assistant who escorted us down a broad corridor that led behind a stage that had been constructed in the main arena. Noise from the crowd already gathered there echoed through the hallway. The tension was palpable and we all whispered nervously, wondering how we'd look when the cameras caught us, if our friends back home would see us, and whether the night would turn out as well as we hoped. None of us had ever experienced anything like the event we saw unfolding before us. It was the biggest night of Sarah's political career and the biggest event we'd ever seen. My palms felt damp and clammy as I walked backstage.

Behind the stage we came to a door that led to the green room, a holding area where Sarah made her final preparations before heading out to the platform. The aide leading us through the building paused by the door and waited as we all caught up. When everyone was together and ready, the aide pushed open the door. And there she was—our Sarah—looking as calm and collected as ever, working the room, smiling and hugging everyone. Aunt Colleen stepped forward to greet her, ready with a quick word of encouragement, but Sarah beat her to the punch. "Isn't this fun?" She smiled. I couldn't believe she was that relaxed. We all shared a moment with her, trying to think of something to say, hoping not to distract her too much.

After a few minutes, the aide returned and led us from the room. We followed her back to the corridor and out to the convention floor. I looked around at the arena, packed to the rafters with delegates and supporters, my eyes wide with wonder. Campaign signs hung from the railings above our head and ran all the way around the upper level. In front of us, more signs filled the air as delegates waved them back and forth. Everywhere people were shouting and chanting their favorite campaign slogans. In my mind I thought, *What in the hell am I doing here?*

Just five days before, I'd been in my classroom in Anchorage, teaching and discussing current events with elementary school students. Now, here I was in St. Paul, Minnesota, at the Republican National Convention. Not merely attending as a bystander, but as an honored guest of the party's vice presidential nominee, my sister, Sarah Palin. To say the moment seemed surreal would be an understatement.

The aide led us through the arena and up the steps to our seats directly above the Alaska delegation. We recognized many faces in that group and waved to them all, proud to be with them and not really caring how hokey we might appear. Not long after we were seated, an announcer introduced Sarah and she walked onto the stage. After an enthusiastic greeting from the crowd, she began to speak.

Perhaps it was the size of the crowd, or the fact that she had to devote the first few minutes to introducing her family, but for whatever reason, the words seemed forced and the cadence labored. I leaned forward and whispered in my father's ear, "This doesn't sound like Sarah." He just nodded and kept his eyes focused on her. I leaned back in my chair and continued to listen, but what I heard was not at all like the Sarah we knew.

After she introduced our parents, the speech began to pick up. Then, near the ten-minute mark, she mentioned that she'd been a hockey mom who signed up for the PTA to make her child's public education better. A group from the Alaska delegation picked up the phrase "hockey mom" and began chanting it over and over, waving hand-lettered signs in time with their voices. The interruption broke Sarah's delivery. Rather than let the moment pass, though, she grinned. "I love those hockey moms. You know what they say is the difference between a hockey mom and a pit bull?...Lipstick." The crowd responded well and she relished the moment. And our Sarah—the one we'd known all our lives—finally took the stage.

Later, when we were with her again in the green room, she told us the teleprompter got ahead of her and was running the pages out of sequence with her delivery. She knew the text well enough to continue but had to disregard the screens. Doing that freed her from the written pages and let her convey the ideas instead of simply reading the text—using her own voice and her own style to deliver the content with passion and conviction. The speech was a rousing success and launched the McCain-Palin campaign into a period of phenomenal popularity.

In the weeks that followed, we watched—sometimes up close and sometimes from a distance—as she wrestled with the rigors of life on the campaign trail and the stresses of being the newest member of a campaign team that had jelled months before. We also watched as the media and liberal pundits ripped into her record, experience, and character. The picture they painted of her was so far from the truth as to be unrecognizable. In the process, many in the country lost sight of the real Sarah.

Our town of Wasilla, Alaska, is a long way from the podium at the Republican National Convention and a long way from the style of a presidential campaign. We live in a region dominated by oil-field workers, commercial fishermen, hunters, military families, and the ordinary people who make America great. Most national politicians live in a world far removed from ours. Yet

Sarah made that trek from where we were—both as a community and as a family—to become a legitimate contender for national office, facing a future filled with the promise of even more opportunities to come. How she made that journey is a tale much bigger than the story of a single person. It's a tale of family, faith, determination, and hard work. Of friendship and loyalty in a community that blossomed in an era when "yes we can" actually meant something.

When she was First Lady, Hillary Clinton wrote a book about children in America and how she thought government could help them. The title of that book was a play on the African proverb "It takes a village to raise a child." I'm not a big fan of Hillary Clinton, but I am a schoolteacher and I know we are all influenced by family, friends, and the community where we live. Sarah is no different. Her character was not formed in a vacuum but in the context of the lives of those whom she knew and loved and who loved her in return.

So, if you want to know Sarah Palin, the real Sarah, our Sarah, you have to understand the places, people, and events that shaped her. And you have to talk to the people who know her best.

I have been blessed to have been raised in this last frontier.

Sarah Palin

CHAPTER 2

Alaska

At the last possible moment, the avalanche split in half and swept past me on either side, leaving me untouched. I've never seen that happen—before or since.
CHUCK HEATH SR.

From the windows near my dining table, I can look out across a broad, glacial valley toward the Chugach Mountains. Tall and majestic, they tower into the sky along the eastern side of Knik Arm in the upper reaches of Cook Inlet, north of Anchorage. On a clear day, the sky above the peaks is as blue as any you've ever seen. Golden streaks of sunshine paint the tallest peaks with brilliant and vivid colors. In the winter, the mountains are covered with snow. Wind roars down the valley and howls around the base of those mountains with the force of a hurricane. In the summer, the mountains are lush with wildflowers, goatsbeard, and prickly rosebud.

A little way up the valley to the east I can see Pioneer Peak. Named in honor of New Deal colonists who came to settle the valley in the 1930s, it rises almost seven thousand feet above the Knik River. In the spring I often stand on our deck and scan the slopes through my spotting scope, watching herds of sheep as they scamper up the saddle near the top.

I climbed that mountain once as part of a mountaineering class. By then I had climbed many mountains, but I needed credit from a class to satisfy the annual continuing education requirements for teacher certification. A friend offered to give me the credits I needed from his course on mountain climbing. I had no choice but to take it. The final project for the class was a climb up Pioneer Peak. Our class consisted of university students, a few professionals like me, four guys from a nearby Army installation, my son, Chuck Jr., and my daughter Heather, who came along for the fun of it.

After a few days of classroom instruction we gathered at the base of Pioneer Peak and set out for the top. My friend, Dave Johnston, once ran from the base of the mountain to the top in a little over two hours. Our pace was considerably slower. We took two days.

With most mountains, there's an easy way and a hard way to reach the summit. Pioneer Peak has a hard way, and a harder way. We chose the more difficult path, a course that took us up the face of the mountain. Through part of the trip, our ascent was almost vertical and as physically taxing as anything I've ever attempted. By the time we reached the final push for the top, two of the Army guys were exhausted. They waited and watched from below while the rest of us clawed our way up. I think it was a little embarrassing for them, being bested by the mountain and a sixth-grade science teacher, but they were wise not to push on. People have died climbing that peak.

Alaska is like that—unsurpassed beauty on the one hand; raw, untamed wilderness on the other; and all of it as close as the view from your own home. It's a place where breathtaking scenes greet you at every turn, and a place where death is never far away, especially in the winter.

We lost a friend, Aaron Arthur, a few years ago in a massive avalanche at Turnagain Pass, a popular location south of Anchorage on the Kenai Peninsula. People from the valley near our home go there in the winter to ski and ride their snowmachines. "Snowmachine" is the Alaskan term for snowmobile. Aaron was an avid fan of snowmachines.

Snowmachiners are a rambunctious bunch and often push life in the wilderness to the limit. Todd Palin, Sarah's husband, rides in the annual Iron Dog race, a two-thousand-mile snowmachine race through the bush country from Big Lake, through Nome, and ending in Fairbanks. Part endurance, part speed, racers blast across the snow at speeds near a hundred miles an hour. Many of the riders suffer frostbite before they reach the finish line. Others find the trail much more challenging. Todd once completed the last four hundred miles with a broken arm.

The snowmachiners who frequent Turnagain Pass don't travel that fast, but they like to push things to the limit. One of their favorite games is called "high-marking"—riding up the face of a slope until the snowmachine can't go any farther, then arcing down to the base in a challenge to see who can climb the highest. It's fun, but it's also dangerous. Those beautiful snow-covered mountains can turn deadly in an instant, as they did for Aaron and five others that day when their high-marking set off a devastating avalanche. It roared down the mountain, burying everything and everyone in its path beneath a massive layer of snow.

The first five bodies were located within a few days, but Aaron was nowhere to be found. I joined a team of volunteers and spent weeks probing the snow with long metal poles, trying to locate him. Aaron's parents set up camp in a motor home in the parking lot below the pass and vowed not to leave until we found him. Fifty-three days later, as winter turned to spring and the sun began to melt the snow, Aaron's brother-in-law spotted something blue sticking out from the crust. It was the sleeve of Aaron's parka. His body was frozen solid.

When the state troopers arrived, they wanted to airlift the body into Anchorage and perform an autopsy to determine the cause of death. Aaron's parents were livid. It was obvious what had happened to him. No one needed a physiological explanation to understand the cause of his demise. After a heated argument, the troopers relented and we propped Aaron's frozen body at the table inside his parents' motor home. Chuck Jr. and Aaron's parents sat with him for the ride into town and talked to him all the way, recalling the things he'd said and done in his much-too-short life. Someone remembered his last words were "Livin' the dream!"

Aaron's not the first person who came to Alaska in search of a dream, only to find that dream cost them the ultimate price. I've come close to death myself, and it wasn't from anything as extreme as high-marking with a snowmachine.

The mountains of Alaska are filled with flocks of ptarmigan. A small bird in the grouse family, they are gray-brown in color through spring and summer, but in winter they turn white. As soon as my children were old enough to negotiate the mountain trails near our home, I took them hunting. Ptarmigan were one of our favorite game birds. Sarah learned to shoot by plinking birds on the mountain slopes. She doesn't have much time for hunting anymore, but she still shoots skeet with her friends at the range not far from town.

One day in the winter, while hunting ptarmigan with my friend Brad Snodgrass, we shot a number of birds that landed on a snowy mountainside, one a lot like the mountain where our friend Aaron played with his snowmachine. I didn't like the angle of the slope and there was a large cornice above us—a ridgeline where the wind had blown away the snow, hollowing out a crusted over-hang of snow and ice. We were skiing that day with long cross-country skis and carried full packs on our backs. In spite of those limitations, Brad was sure we could dash onto the slope, scoop up the birds, and get back before anything happened. We both knew better, but we made a run for it anyway. Just as I suspected, our ski strokes across the snow sent vibrations up the slope and the cornice gave way. A wall of heavy white snow thundered down the mountain toward us.

Unlike what you might imagine, an avalanche is not a gen-tle slow slide. The snow cascades down the mountain, gathering momentum as it goes, often reaching speeds in excess of a hun-dred miles per hour. Wind pushes ahead of the growing wall of snow, ripping the tops off trees in its path. When the snow moves like that, its force is measured in tons.

One-third of those caught in an avalanche are killed outright by the trauma of the event—they're hit by slabs of ice, broken tree limbs, and other flying debris, or their bodies are ripped apart by the force of the snow. Another third are buried and suffocate. It's a fantasy to think one can dig himself out of a firmly packed encase-ment. Those who survive say that they couldn't even move their fingers, open their eyes, or expand their chest enough to breathe. I've attended classes that suggest you can survive by "swimming" on top of the snow. That's almost impossible. In reality, the only way to escape is by moving laterally.

That day with Brad, I had skied too far out on the slope to get back to safety and, to make matters worse, in my effort to move quickly I fell through the crust into waist-deep snow. Brad, who was much closer to the edge, made it out of the way. All I could do was stand there and watch as the snow came toward me.

I remember thinking things like, *Here I am, in a predicament that*

I have preached to others they should avoid. And, *This can't be happening to me. I know all there is to know about avalanches.* As irony would have it, at the time this happened I was teaching an avalanche safety course. Yet, there I was, staring certain death squarely in the eye. Brad told me later that he was marking my spot as best he could, in hopes of later recovering my body. Even he was certain I was going to die.

Seconds later, a gust of wind swept across my face. Driven by the onrushing snow, it felt cold and crisp against my skin. A slab came toward my head. I ducked to one side and dodged it. Then, at the last possible moment, the avalanche split in half and swept past me on either side, leaving me untouched. I've never seen that happen—before or since.

Alaska is a place of adventure, which means it's a place where humans face the very real possibility of death or serious injury. I've lost four friends to avalanches and spent days searching for each of them. I've lost friends to other tragedies too.

Our region of the continent is home to all three North American bears—polar bears, black bears, and brown (grizzly) bears. Though encounters with bears are statistically rare, those encounters often prove deadly. Marcie Trent and her son were killed when they surprised a bear on a trail near Anchorage. Marcie was an accomplished long-distance runner and held four world records in her age group. She died almost instantly when the bear's claw struck her neck. Alaska is bear country, a fact my family and I have witnessed firsthand.

When the children were young, we took them on a caribou hunt. I killed a caribou the first day and we hauled it back to our camp. With everyone helping, we gutted the animal and tied it to the top of the car, thinking it would be safe there. That night, I was awakened by a bear that was standing beside the car, gnawing on the caribou carcass. I wanted to shoot it, but the kids were sleeping in a tent that I had pitched for them just a few feet away. I knew I could hit the bear but I wasn't sure I could kill it with a single shot. If I wounded it, the bear would land on the tent. I managed to scare it away, but a few hours later it returned. After I chased it away a second time, we gathered up the kids and spent the remainder of the night in the car with an up-close view of the bear as it returned once more to dine on the caribou. Two days later, a hunter from the Fish and Game Commission killed the bear. It was a twenty-eight-year-old grizzly with a record of terrorizing camps and cabins.

During Sarah's last year as governor, she and Todd invited Sally and me to go with them on an official visit to the McNeil River State Game Sanctuary, one of the best bear sanctuaries on the continent. Located on the upper end of the Alaska Peninsula, the McNeil River is about thirty-five miles long, flowing from McNeil Lake in the interior of the peninsula down to McNeil Cove at the coast near the mouth of Cook Inlet. In the summertime, a strong tidal surge pushes salmon up the rivers and streams all along the inlet. As a result, McNeil River has a tremendous salmon run. Those salmon, in turn, attract a large number of brown bears, making the sanctuary one of the most popular wildlife attractions in the state.

While gorging themselves on salmon, the bears along McNeil River pay no attention to humans. During our visit, we sat just a few yards away from them and watched as they snagged fish from the water with their paws and dove beneath the surface to catch them with their mouths. More than forty bears were gathered there that day.

At one point, the bears wandered as close as three feet from where we were seated. The ground shook when they walked by.

Armed guides from the Fish and Game Commission stood near us to make sure the bears didn't harm us, but no one has ever been injured by a bear attack there. Just to be safe, when we arrived I told the guards that if a bear got on top of me they should shoot it and not worry about hitting me. I'd rather take my chances with their marksmanship skills than with the bear.

Bears are a challenge to life in the wild, but they aren't the only risk we face in Alaska. A few years ago, I was on a moose hunt with my friends Adrian Lane, Dave Reeves, Craig Lyndon, and Mike Hodsdon. We hauled our four-wheelers out to a spot off the Denali Highway not far from the Maclaren River, then rode into the woods. At the river we loaded our gear and four-wheelers onto an airboat operated by our friend Fred Haynes. He ferried us across to the opposite side and we continued on another ten or fifteen miles. Doing that put us well beyond the area covered by typical hunters. We've hunted like that for the past twenty years.

About a week into the hunt we received a call on the satellite phone from Dave's wife. They had an emergency at home and he needed to get back to town quickly. Dave packed his gear and prepared to leave. For safety, we never traveled alone, so Adrian and I accompanied him on our four-wheelers back to the river crossing. Fred was waiting for us when we arrived. Dave drove his four-wheeler onto the airboat, then took a seat near the back. Normally, Fred added ballast to the stern of the boat to counteract the weight of the four-wheeler lashed to the bow, in order to make the boat sit level in the water. This time, because he was in a hurry to get across the river, he chose to make the trip without the ballast.

The Maclaren River is a glacial river. The water is cold and moves swiftly. That day, the water was particularly high and moved unusually fast. As Fred turned the boat to make the crossing, a wave caught the bow and forced it down beneath the surface.

The Heath farm in Hope, Idaho, 1948.

Chuck Heath Sr.'s first fish, a bass caught off the pier in Santa Barbara, California.

The Heath family—Marie, Carol, Chuck, and Charlie—in North Hollywood, California, 1946.

The Sheeran family: Mother Helen, Kate, Clem, Peggy, Pat, Sally, Colleen, and Mike.

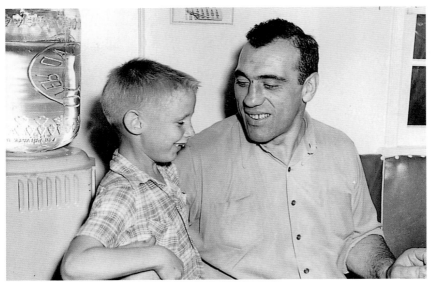

Chuck Sr. with heavyweight boxing champion Primo Carnera, 1946.

Heath family vacation trip from North Hollywood to Idaho, 1947.

Chuck Jr., age 4; Sarah, age 2; and Heather, age 3; in Skagway, Alaska.

Chuck Sr. and Sally Heath in a remote cabin in the Chugach Mountains.

The Heath kids—Heather, Molly, Chuck, and Sarah— Eagle River, Alaska, 1971.

Chuck Sr. with Chuck, Sarah, and Heather and dog at the Tank Farm home in Skagway, Alaska, 1965.

Chuck Sr. as a sheep hunt guide in the Wrangell Mountains in 1972. He carried a hundred-pound pack filled with camp and hunting gear, sheep meat, and horns.

The Heath kids with one of their exotic pets, a boa constrictor named Junior, 1971.

Sarah and Heather on their skis.

Sarah, a sophomore in high
school, holding the regional
first-place cross-country
trophy.

Sarah shooting hoops
on the dirt court at
home in Wasilla.

Sarah and Molly with
Coach Dad and the
Wasilla High School
cross-country team,
1981.

The Heath family,
Christmas 1980.

Heather Heath;
Kurt Bruce; Molly
Heath McCann;
Sally Heath; Chuck
Heath Sr.; Sarah;
Chuck Heath Jr.;
Todd Palin; and
Track, age 2; 1991

Todd and Sarah,
high school
graduation, 1982.

Sarah celebrates her BS degree at the University of Idaho, 1987.

Sarah running her leg of a fifty-mile race over Hatcher Pass, 1995.

Already overloaded in front with the four-wheeler, the bow sank quickly. The force of the current caught the boat and sent it tumbling end over end downstream. They had lifejackets, but rather than wearing them, the jackets lay at the bottom of the boat.

Dave was thrown free of the craft and swam hard trying to keep his head above the surface. He did his best but the cold water quickly sapped his strength. Water that cold feels like needles stabbing your skin. It also rapidly depletes body heat. In just a few short minutes, Dave was exhausted and in serious trouble. He told us later that he reached a point where he was certain he'd made his last stroke. Prepared to die, his body sank into the water. At that very moment, his feet touched bottom. Dave is six and a half feet tall. If he'd been any shorter he would have drowned, but that day he made it safely to the riverbank, saved by his height. Not long after he pulled himself from the water, two men in an airboat found him, wet and hypothermic. They built a fire and helped him get warm.

Fred was not so fortunate. We spent the remainder of the day searching for him, the boat, and the four-wheeler, but found no sign of them. Soldiers from a National Guard unit arrived late in the afternoon to help. State troopers finally arrived the next morning. We located the four-wheeler about a mile downstream. Someone found Fred's body on a sandbar. They never found the boat.

Alaska is a place of extremes, a characteristic that is readily discernible to even the casual visitor. We have bitterly cold winters; twenty-hour summer days, followed by twenty-hour winter nights. The terrain is marked by imposing mountain ranges and remote wilderness areas that never have been touched by human footprints. Seeing it for the first time you might think the region produces hard people with little heart or empathy for others. Nothing could be further from the truth. In contrast to the often harsh weather conditions and challenging terrain, the people of Alaska are warm, friendly, and have an infectious, though ironic, sense of humor. Nothing exemplifies that spirit better than the story of Louie Liken and the Sour Toe Cocktail.

Back in the 1920s, Louie worked in the Alaskan bush as a hunter and trapper. One winter he suffered frostbite on his big toe. With true Alaskan grit and determination, he amputated the toe himself to prevent gangrene. Rather than dispose of the toe, he pickled it in a bottle of rum.

After Louie died, a friend named Bill Holmes cleaned out the cabin and found the bottle with the toe inside. He took the bottle to the Eldorado Hotel in Dawson City, Yukon, where it sat on a shelf in the hotel bar until one night when a woman saw it and took a drink from the bottle. Thus began the tradition of the Sour Toe Cocktail—a drink consumed with the well-preserved human toe resting at the bottom of the glass.

As with most other things, rules developed about what counted as a true Sour Toe Cocktail. At first the drink was required to be alcoholic, and patrons had to completely consume it in various ways and forms. These days the drink can be of any variety and there is only a single simple rule contained in the oft-repeated phrase, "You can drink it fast, you can drink it slow, but the lips gotta touch the toe." Touching the toe with your lips is all that's required, but some have been more enthusiastic than others in the way they did it.

Eventually, the toe passed through several owners and now resides at the Downtown Hotel in Dawson City. However, the current toe is not the original one. As of the last time I checked, the one now used for the cocktail is toe number seven. Four were swallowed by overly enthusiastic drinkers and two others were stolen. Various donors have supplied replacements, the most recent coming from a man who included a specific bequest of his toes in his will.

You might not share this kind of Alaskan humor, but many of us have a certificate to prove we are official Sour Toe Cocktail drinkers. My wife, Sally, and I drank one with Sarah and Todd at the end of the Over the Top snowmachine trek, an annual two-hundred-mile snowmachine ride through the bush from Tok to Chicken, Alaska, then across the river into Dawson City. We have the certificates to prove it. Our friends Adrian and Marilyn Lane were with us.

A few years ago, my son spent the Fourth of July in Manley Hot Springs. It's a small mining town about 150 miles northeast of Fairbanks. Independence Day is still an occasion for celebration in rural Alaska, and Manley hosts one of the best. Townspeople gather at the local park for games and races. Natives from villages like Tanana and Minto come into town. Gold miners leave their claims and join celebrants in the village to eat, listen to music, and swap stories.

On this particular Fourth of July, a bar called the Roadhouse held a community barbecue. Everyone from miles around showed up. A band, featuring Alaska's own Frank Gurtler, kept the dance floor packed. In the middle of one of the songs, a big burly ex-Marine named Buzz Burr suddenly collapsed on the floor. The music stopped and when the crowd realized Buzz wasn't breathing, two men began performing CPR. One man did the chest compressions while the other breathed into Buzz's mouth. This went on for ten minutes or so, and then my son took a turn. He tilted Buzz's head back and blew air into his lungs, watching his chest rise and fall with each breath. After what seemed like half an hour there still was no response from Buzz. Finally, everyone realized he was dead and there was nothing else they could do for him. Someone called the state troopers, but since Manley was in a remote location, it took a while for the troopers to respond.

Everyone in the bar had been watching this scene play out and when they realized Buzz was gone, someone grabbed his baseball cap and, in a gesture of honor and respect, hung it on a rack above the bar. Someone else found a blanket and spread it over the body. No one wanted to move his body before the troopers arrived, so they left him lying right there in the middle of the dance floor. Then the band started playing again and everyone continued dancing around his body. In between songs, people told their best Buzz stories and drank a toast to him. It was a great way for him to go out. He was with his best friends, in his favorite place, listening to great music and dancing with beautiful women.

That's Alaska—a place of wonder and beauty, a place of danger and grace. As majestic as the towering mountains and as unforgiving as the cascading avalanche. It remains the last American frontier, where brain and brawn confront raw, unvarnished nature in a struggle that shapes them both. And it was to that Alaska that I brought my family during the summer of 1964. What we found there made us who we are today. For Sally, me, and our children—Chuck Jr., Heather, Sarah, and Molly—it was a life-changing adventure. One that brought us face-to-face with nature, tragedy, death, and opportunity, and in the process made us more alive than we ever could have imagined.

The first people to settle in the valley where we live arrived there on a quest. Most of them came seeking their fortune from the natural resources of the region. Russian trappers came in the 1700s. In the 1800s, someone discovered gold in Willow Creek, about twenty-five miles north of Wasilla, and gold miners flocked to the area. During World War I, men came to mine the coal deposits that lay north of Palmer. At the height of the Great

Depression, the federal government created the Matanuska Colony and resettled more than two hundred families in the valley. They came from Michigan, Wisconsin, and Minnesota—regions hit unusually hard by the economic collapse.

Though we came many years later, we encountered similar challenges of climate. terrain, and inaccessibility that confronted those early settlers. Like them, we came to Alaska in search of a better life and found it in the struggles we faced.

On the map, we moved from Idaho to Skagway, then from Skagway to Wasilla. In the broader scope of things, the personal journey we began with that physical step took us much farther than any map could measure. Some people thought our move to Alaska was the result of a whim—that we were going off on a lark and only decided to leave on the spur of the moment. I'm sure others thought we'd lost our minds. Actually, our move was part of a much bigger story, one that encompassed the lives of several generations and had been a long time in the making.

Alaska kids grow up fishing the state's three million lakes in the summer and racing across them in winter on snowmachines, kicking up rooster tails of snow.

Sarah Palin

CHAPTER 3

Charlie

*For some reason, Grandpa got the idea it would be fun to fly
a biplane upside down over Hollywood Boulevard.*
CHUCK HEATH JR.

Our family history in America stretches all the way back to
the landing of the *Mayflower* at Plymouth Rock. I heard
stories about that from childhood but never knew the details of our
lineage until after Sarah was nominated as John McCain's running mate in 2008. During the months that followed, researchers
traced her ancestry and made it available to the public as part of the
political vetting process. That sense of historical perspective didn't
influence us much as children. Most of what shaped us—from a
family history perspective—began with our paternal grandfather.
His friends called him Charlie. We knew him as Grandpa.

Grandpa was born Francis Oriel Heath in 1901, in Chicago,
Illinois. His mother died the following year and shortly after that
his father took him to California, where they settled in the Los
Angeles area. A year later, his father married a woman known to
the family only as Agnes. They raised the boy who would become
our grandfather under the name Charles F. Heath. He was an
adult before he learned that Agnes, whom he'd known throughout
childhood as his mother, wasn't his biological parent.

As a general rule, Grandpa refused to talk much about his father, but from the few memories that have survived I'm sure their relationship must have been tumultuous. He attended elementary school, then dropped out and went to work. His father had owned a bicycle shop in Chicago, but in Los Angeles he operated a radio and electrical supply business. The two worked it together with Grandpa helping out in sales.

Selling electrical supplies helped pay the bills, but that's all it was—a way to make a living. Grandpa's first love was sports and, second to that, photography. He was a quick learner and taught himself to use a camera. A naturally gifted salesman, with a penchant for being in the right place at the right time, he combined his two interests—sports and photography—and began covering events in the Los Angeles area. It wasn't long before he left the electrical business for a career as a photographer. He took pictures of many things, but most of the photographs that survive today are of sports events and celebrities, primarily people involved with boxing and wrestling.

The events he covered were local. Boxing and wrestling at the Grand Olympic Auditorium, Hollywood Legion Stadium, or Wrigley Field (Los Angeles). Midget auto racing at Loyola High School Stadium and Gilmore Stadium. College football at the Rose Bowl. With its moderate climate and thriving motion-picture business, Los Angeles attracted many national celebrities, and Grandpa took full advantage of that.

By then he was married to our grandmother, Marie Brandt, and they often invited sports celebrities to their home. They entertained the likes of heavyweight boxing champions James J. Jeffries, Joe Louis, and Primo Carnera, along with professional wrestling's first superstars, Gorgeous George and Man Mountain Dean. They also were friends with Barney Oldfield, an early automobile-racing celebrity, and many lesser-known boxing figures such as Manuel Ortiz and Tony Olivera, both of whom fought in the bantamweight division.

Covering sports events opened other opportunities too. George Temple Jr., a professional wrestler whom Grandpa photographed many times, was an older brother to the childhood actress Shirley Temple. As a rising young Hollywood star, Shirley needed publicity photographs. George suggested Grandpa for the job and it wasn't long before he was one of her photographers too.

An expanding array of friendships also gave him the opportunity to work in the film industry. He appeared as an extra in a number of motion pictures, including several of the popular children's short comedy films in the *Our Gang* series, episodes of which were later syndicated for television as *The Little Rascals*. As a child I was fascinated when he told me about how excited the kids became when action in a scene called for them to break a window. The glass was made of sugar and after it broke, all the kids scrambled to eat the pieces.

As a young man, Grandpa watched the aviation industry flourish and, like many of that era, he was intrigued by airplanes. Never one to pass up an opportunity for adventure, he obtained a pilot's license and took to the skies above Los Angeles. Not long after that, he got the idea that it would be fun to fly a biplane upside down over Hollywood Boulevard. The commotion that followed was a little too much for the authorities, and an investigation was launched to determine the pilot's identity. It wasn't difficult to figure out who was flying the plane. We have a photograph of Dad as a young boy standing beside a plane when he went for his first flight. The tail number was registered to a Waco GXE, a biplane with three seats that was manufactured in 1928. I like to imagine it's the same one Grandpa flew.

In 1938, when our father was born, the family, including Dad's older sister, Carol, lived in a small house on Farmdale Avenue in North Hollywood. Dad spent the first ten years of his life in the raucous world of Hollywood at its golden age, a time that coincided with many of the events my grandfather covered as a sports photographer. Together, the two of them palled around Los Angeles—Grandpa in his forties, Dad just a kid. They saw many of the memorable sporting events of their day and met sports celebrities most people could only admire from afar. Some of Dad's earliest memories are from events at Grand Olympic Auditorium, accompanying his father into the locker room after boxing matches, and seeing wrestlers who were enemies in the ring laughing and joking afterward. Often, on the way home, Grandpa stopped off at a café or bar for a drink with a few of the boxers and wrestlers. Dad, though only a child, was right there with him.

When he wasn't with Grandpa at an event, Dad walked with his friends over to Republic Studios, seven or eight blocks away, and slipped under the fence to watch movies in the making. Republic made low-budget, black-and-white cowboy films and was home to Roy Rogers and Gene Autry. Dad and his friends watched as the action unfolded in Republic's soundstage studio buildings or on the lot outside.

With the outbreak of World War II, Grandpa felt a sense of duty to participate in defending the country. Well past the draft age, he volunteered for service in the Navy and was inducted as a photojournalist. Much to his dismay, a few months later he was granted an honorable discharge and sent home. War, as it turned out, really was a young man's battle.

Like many American families, they spent the war years learning to live in a rationed economy. Dad and his neighborhood friends sold war bond stamps. A scaled-down version of war bonds, customers purchased stamps, often for pennies each, which were placed in a booklet. When the booklet was filled, it could be redeemed for an actual bond. The program was targeted toward children. Dad and his friends received free movie tickets for every book they filled.

By the end of the war, Los Angeles and the neighborhood in North Hollywood had changed. Industries associated with the war effort brought thousands of new people to the area and life moved at a frenetic pace. At the same time, the classic era of motion pictures was coming to a close. Television was on the rise.

That same year, Dad caught his first fish off the Santa Barbara Pier, a sea bass that weighed about five pounds. Carol was with him and for several days they carried it around like a trophy. Catching that first fish might not sound like much, but it ignited the adventuresome nature already well formed in Dad's soul. Like many young boys, he had dreamed of fishing and hunting for most of his life but, living in Los Angeles, those dreams seemed far-fetched. Grandpa was infected with the same idea, and between them they began to discuss locations where they might explore their growing interest in the outdoors. Before long, the talk turned serious and our grandparents began to consider a move to the country.

Over the following weeks and months they took several vacations, wandering through Northern California and traveling east into Nevada. Our grandparents didn't know much about roughing it but they did their best to make the trips an adventure, camping by the side of the road and eating meals prepared over a portable stove. Most nights they slept in the car.

In the spring of 1948, they drove through the northern tier of states on a trip that took them to Sandpoint, Idaho. At the time, most of the state was still rural and untamed. Lake Pend Oreille, a beautiful expanse some sixty-five miles long, was only just being discovered as a sportsman's favorite. Timber and logging were the mainstays of the economy. Tourism had not yet become the region's primary attraction. As a result, the area retained much of its rustic charm while also providing most of the conveniences Americans were beginning to expect—electricity, running water, and paved roads.

After exploring the town and surrounding countryside for a few days, they settled on a house and farm near the town of Hope, a small community on the east side of Lake Pend Oreille, about fifteen miles outside Sandpoint. They made the move that summer. Dad was ten years old, and he couldn't have been happier.

In human relationships, drawing causal connections from one generation to the next seems a little risky. However, when I look at our family, that move—from California to Idaho, from a life focused on sports photography to one focused on living an outdoor life—marked a major turning point for Dad, one that had a profound effect on the generations that followed.

Like ripples from a rock striking the surface of a pond, relocating to Idaho and the life it afforded sent ever-expanding waves through the succeeding generations. From a fish caught on a dock in Santa Barbara, to a string of fish from Lake Pend Oreille, to hunting deer and elk, first our grandfather, then our father, and then the children and grandchildren were captured by a spirit of adventure. Not that all of us have become hunters, but we all have found our lives propelled by a force that compels us to press against our comfort zone in whatever we do. When we run, we want to run faster. When we hunt, we want to nab larger game. When we fish, we want to catch one more. To *really* run, *really* hunt, *really* fish, always pressing forward for an experience more authentic than the last. That same progression is evident in Sarah's life.

During her senior year in college, Sarah worked as an intern at KTUU, a television station in Anchorage. When she completed her degree, the station hired her full-time. She reported on local sporting events and helped prepare stories for others on the staff. Some of those tasks were menial, but she had a goal of becoming a national reporter with ESPN and she was doing everything she could to make it happen. Finally, on Sunday, January 31, 1988, she appeared on the air for the first time as the sports anchor. It was the evening broadcast following the Super Bowl. I'm not sure how many people watched the show. She was given the anchor duty because everyone else was away watching the football game. She didn't mind. Becoming a studio anchor was one of the things she needed to do in order to move up in her career. She was just glad to be there and have time in front of the camera. John Hernandez, the sports director who hired her, remembered she seemed a little nervous but she completed the show without mishap and the station was satisfied with her work. Anchoring that newscast, like other aspects of her work at the station, took her to the edge of her comfort level. Rather than resist, she pressed forward. As a result, she grew in confidence and ability.

Several years later, when she agreed to run for an open seat on the Wasilla City Council, Sarah once again was pushed beyond her comfort zone. To get elected, she would have to speak in public. That much she could handle. She'd spent hours in front of a camera and knew how to handle herself before an audience. Other aspects of the task—addressing voters face-to-face, soliciting the help of supporters, and holding her own with the male-dominated council after the election—pushed her toward experiences she'd never encountered. Like everything else, she dove into the task with energy and determination.

Her experience on the council showed her that to really effect change in city government she would have to serve as mayor. Although she was young and had served only one term, she had the confidence to believe she could do the mayor's job. In addition, she had the vision to see that winning the post was possible. Neither of those things had seemed likely when she first ran for city council. Having attained that initial position, the mayor's office didn't seem so overwhelming.

Being mayor forced her to deal with larger issues. Road and sewer construction, improvements in the police department, relocation of the city's airport, development of the Menard Center (a multiuse sports complex), and the bond issue to pay for it once again nudged her to the edge of her comfort zone. Rather than shrink back, she pressed forward, mastered the issues, and grew in the process. From the mayor's office, statewide politics appeared less formidable.

In 2002, buoyed by her success as mayor, Sarah ran for lieutenant governor in the Republican primary. That campaign pushed her further into politics than she'd gone before. She learned to campaign throughout the state rather than simply in our own town and to address issues beyond those that affected only our region. It wasn't comfortable, but it was a necessary step in the progression toward politics at the next level.

After a term on the city council, two terms as mayor, and a statewide campaign, running for governor wasn't as scary as it might have seemed years before. Many people thought she was crazy for trying. Some were surprised by her move into politics altogether. It wasn't much like anything she'd done in life to that point. Yet to those of us who understood her best, each campaign seemed like the next logical thing.

In 2008, when Sarah became the Republican Party's nominee for vice president, things really got crazy. Many of our friends and even some of our family members were caught completely off guard. Some people who knew us but lived out of state didn't even know she was governor. I wasn't prepared for her move up to national politics, but I realized at each step in her career she'd come to a vision of the next level. She couldn't have foreseen the run for vice president from the council chamber in Wasilla, but she could see the next thing and that's what she focused on, taking the next step.

All of that started with our grandparents' move from North Hollywood to the tiny community of Hope, outside Sandpoint, Idaho. Like a rock dropped in the lake, Charlie's sense of adventure, of pressing forward toward living the life he dreamed, moved him, then Dad, then each of us to do the same, to live against the edge of hardship rather than retreat from it, and to embrace a life of adventure and possibility.

Dad's childhood seemed to me painful and lonely.

Sarah Palin

CHAPTER 4

Idaho, Sally . . . and Children

*I think about that sometimes—the town's first female doctor
delivering Alaska's first female governor, who became the first
female candidate on the Republican Party's national ticket.*
CHUCK HEATH SR.

When we arrived in Idaho, Charlie set up his photography business in one of the rooms of the house, but we were new to the area and lived out in Hope, almost fifteen miles from Sandpoint. Another photographer, Ross Hall, already had a business there with a large studio on First Avenue and an established clientele. Hall also was gaining a national reputation with works published in *National Geographic* and *LIFE* magazines. Opportunities for freelance sports photography, which had been my father's specialty in California, were few and far between. Portrait photography, which had been a steady though smaller part of his business, was all but unheard of in our small community. To help make ends meet, he took a job driving a school bus. Mom, who had been a teacher in California, wasn't certified to teach in Idaho, and had to take classes to get approved by the state for a teaching position. During those first years in Idaho, eating meant living off the land, literally.

That year I got my first gun, a Benjamin pellet rifle, and

started bringing home grouse for dinner. A few months later, at the age of eleven, I received a Stevens .22 caliber rifle. With it I added rabbits to go with the grouse. I took that rifle with me to school every morning and kept it in the coat closet. At the end of the day I walked home on the power line right of way and hunted my way back to the house.

When I was twelve, I received my first high-powered rifle and soon after that bagged my first deer. Over the next several years I shot many more, including five from my own bedroom window. Before I was sixteen years old, I had already shot bear and elk, too. Charlie saw that I enjoyed hunting and knew I was good at it, but ammunition was expensive. He allotted me a certain number of bullets each month and held me accountable for their use. It was my obligation to make certain none of them was wasted and that each of them counted toward edible game.

In the spring and summer, I spent most days fishing at the lake. Lake Pend Oreille, just down the hill from our house, was sixty-five miles long. It covered 148 square miles and reached depths of more than 1,100 feet. So deep, in fact, that the US Navy established a submarine training base there during World War II. The lake teemed with fish that were easy to catch. A local processor paid ten cents each for Kokanee salmon and on some days I made more than ten dollars.

The school at Hope included only grades one through eight but had a thriving sports program. I played baseball, basketball, and football through eighth grade. We had some good teams during those years, but it was a rural school, which meant the physical facilities weren't always the best. Most kids today would cringe at the thought of playing games in the places we played. Instead of complaining, we turned those inadequacies into strengths.

Baseball games were played on a field that included a four-foot drop at the third-base line and a tree in right field. We used both to our advantage. The drop-off kept us in a few games when left-fielders from opposing teams stumbled and fell chasing foul balls that otherwise would have been caught for outs. The tree in right field gave the fielder a shady place to wait for the inning to come to an end. Almost no one hit the ball in that direction. We won most of our games, but the worst thing that happened wasn't the few games we lost. One day in eighth grade during a game against the team from Kootenai, our pitcher, Steve Johnson, collapsed on the mound and died. The memory of it sticks with me to this very day.

If the field gave us a slight advantage in baseball, the gymnasium was like having a sixth player on the basketball team. The backboards were nailed directly to the wall, which meant shooting a layup required an approach from the side with the right kind of finesse. There was no room to run out beneath the board. The wall behind the basket was out of bounds. Walls on either side of the court were close, too. And the ceiling was low, only about two feet higher than the backboard. Many teams we played against held their practices on outdoor courts or in a gym with a high ceiling. They learned to shoot jump shots using the typical arc that sent the ball high into the air and dropped it down through the rim of the basket. If you shot like that in the gym at Hope, the ball would hit the ceiling. Like the walls, the ceiling was out of bounds and prevented many teams from scoring on us.

By the time I completed eighth grade, I was already maturing as an athlete. Football and basketball were the center of my life. I still was required to do chores on the farm, as well as provide the family with meat from hunting, but the competitiveness of organized sports emerged as the driving force in my personality. I loved the challenge of vying for a win. For me there was nothing like the thrill of winning.

At the same time, education was very important to my mother. During junior high and the first two years of high school I was only allowed to participate in sports if I maintained grades at an honor-student level. Those two things—sports and academics—became the hallmarks of my life and the keys to a successful professional career. They emerged to dominate my life as I reached high school age.

Because the school at Hope only went through the eighth grade, to complete my secondary education, I attended Sandpoint High School, about fifteen miles from our home. The school district provided a bus to transport students from Hope and other areas into town, but that only gave me a ride to school in the morning. Through my four years of high school, I competed in football, basketball, and track, which meant I participated in sporting events and practices all year long. Practices and games were held in the afternoon and evening after school was dismissed. By the time they ended, the school bus had long since run its route. My father refused to drive to town to pick me up, which meant I was forced to hitchhike home. Many nights I walked most of the way and didn't arrive home until midnight.

The schedule was tough those first couple of years in high school, but we were blessed with great coaches. Their interest in us, and the example they set, provided inspiration for the rest of our lives. Our football coach, Cotton Barlow, was an Idaho legend.

A native of Sparta, Tennessee, he graduated from Tennessee Tech, where he lettered in football. In World War II he was stationed at Farragut Naval Training Center on Lake Pend Oreille. When the war was over he was discharged from the Navy and took a temporary job as Sandpoint High School's football coach. The job turned into a career that lasted thirty-three years. Under

Coach Barlow's watchful eye, I learned the value of hard work and humility. During the four years I played for him in high school, our team lost only four games. We were a little small, but also fast and tough. Coach Barlow once said of us, "They're not very big, but they're not smart enough to know the difference." We knew the difference. We just didn't care about it and played over our heads in every game.

One of the reasons we did so well was because we had Jerry Kramer at right tackle. He went on to fame as an offensive guard for the Green Bay Packers, where he played for Coach Vince Lombardi. I was a sophomore when he was a senior at Sandpoint. Even in high school, Jerry was big, strong, and fast. Like most of the guys on the team, I was fast but not very big. As a running back, I relied on Jerry to open holes through the defense that allowed me to scamper past defenders and score. Most of the time, Jerry blocked anyone who came near me. Someone asked him recently about me. Jerry replied in a typically terse way. "He worked hard and kept his mouth shut." That summed up my approach to just about everything. Work hard and stick to your own business.

I also did well at track under a coach named Art Gamblin. We didn't think too much of his training technique—he made all of the team, including sprinters, start every practice with a five-mile run—but he was a master at motivation. Later, as a high school coach myself, I borrowed some of his tips. We didn't always have the best athletes, but we entered each meet not only believing we could win, but convinced we couldn't lose. With his help, I set a number of high school records, including a time in the hundred-yard dash that stood for forty years.

While I excelled in sports, life at home deteriorated. As I grew through adolescence, my father became an uncompromising and heavy-handed disciplinarian. During those years, our relationship was marred by physical punishment that included beatings with a rubber hose and, if that was inconvenient, a back-handed slap to the jaw.

As with most budding teenagers, driving was important to me. With a car, I could get around on my own and it seemed like the perfect solution to my schedule problem. Learner's permits could be issued as young as the age of fourteen and I obtained mine in the spring of 1952. That same year, my father acquired a red 1952 MG sports car. It looked sharp, ran fast, and was fun to drive. The two of us motored around the countryside together as I learned to handle a car and dreamed of taking it to school. But when I reached an age that allowed me to drive on my own, my father refused to let me take the car to school. Walking home those cold dark nights from Sandpoint to Hope, tired from practice or a game—knowing there was a car sitting at home—planted a seed of resentment in me that grew to anger and bitterness.

With my sports schedule and commute occupying most of my free time, chores at home went lacking. What little time I did have went to completing schoolwork. Finally, at the end of my sophomore year, my father gave me an ultimatum: "Give up the sports or find someplace else to live." To make matters worse, he sold the MG sports car.

I had been dating a classmate named Sharon Mooney. She lived in Sandpoint, and I had grown very close to her family. When her parents, Gordon and Dorothy, heard about my predicament they offered to let me move in with them. I accepted on the spot. After that, my parents never attended any of my games or track meets. They attended my high school graduation ceremony, primarily because my sister, Carol, graduated that same year, but for the most part, I had very limited contact with them through the remainder of my life.

I've wrestled with how this happened—my father, the consummate sports enthusiast and me, the consummate athlete, unable to bridge my transition from boyhood to manhood. No doubt, he brought with him emotional scars from his own childhood, but that doesn't fully explain how our relationship came to an end, and neither does it account for the men our friends knew us to be. Still, events leading up to my last two years in high school marked a turning point that set the course for the remainder of my life and the course for my family's life as well.

After graduating from high school in Sandpoint, I planned to attend college but lacked the money to enroll. In an effort to solve that problem I joined the Army Reserve—a kind of resourcefulness later mirrored by Sarah when she entered the Miss Wasilla beauty pageant in an effort to win scholarships for college. The Army required me to serve an initial six months on active duty followed by eight years as a reservist. The pay helped toward the expense of college but the time on active duty went by slowly. I longed to be on the football field or in the gym playing basketball.

Soon after I completed the initial six months of active duty, Skip Pennington, the assistant football coach at Columbia Basin College in Pasco, Washington, offered me a football scholarship. He offered one to my friend Ray Carter, too. We accepted immediately and headed to Washington together. Our lives would become even more entwined as the years went by. Ray and his wife, Kris, went to Alaska the year before us and when we moved to Wasilla, I worked for him at two different schools where he was the principal.

The scholarship to Columbia Basin covered room and board, plus books and tuition. For extra money, I swept floors at a nearby high school, washed dishes in the college cafeteria, and drove a school bus, in addition to playing football, attending class, and meeting my Army Reserve obligations.

Columbia Basin was a new junior college with a new athletic program. However, it competed in the Washington Junior College Conference against older, established schools. I played on the football team as a running back but didn't have Jerry Kramer to block for me. Running behind a weaker offensive line, I took far too many hits. By the end of the first season I had dislocated both shoulders and injured a knee, which brought my football career to an end. Unable to continue playing, I lost the athletic scholarship. However, thanks to study habits drilled into me by my mother, my grades qualified me for an academic scholarship and I was able to remain a student. I'm glad I did.

One day in a zoology lab class, I was paired with a girl named Sally Sheeran. Our assignment that day was to prick each other's fingers and take a blood sample. At first, she refused to participate. Ever the gallant and considerate one, I responded by calling her a pansy. I liked her but wanted to date another girl in our class, Linda Mitchell. However, when I asked Linda out, she wanted to go with my roommate instead. Rather than going with me, Linda offered to fix me up for a date with her best friend. Her best friend turned out to be Sally Sheeran. I'm not sure I made a good impression on her—I paid for the movie with a sock full of coins and when I tried to put my arm around her my shoulder popped out of joint—but we continued to date and she took me home to meet her family.

If Sally was impressed, Clem, her father, was not, and neither was the rest of the family. Her sisters deny it now, but when they met me they said, "Sally usually brings all these nice, good-looking guys around. And then there's you." I was an athlete and an adventurer. Not exactly the man they expected for their quiet, demure Sally.

After two years at Columbia Basin, I transferred to Eastern Washington University. Located twenty miles south of Spokane, the school was established in 1882, with a grant from Benjamin Pierce Cheney, a businessman and founder of the company that eventually became American Express. While I continued working toward a bachelor's degree, Sally transferred to a technical college in Spokane and began studying to be a dental assistant. We exchanged an occasional letter but slowly drifted apart.

That was a lean time for me. I had enough money to pay tuition, but none for room and board. I slept in various rooms at the dormitory—first with this friend, then with that one, sometimes sleeping on the floor. From time to time, friends brought me food. One of those who helped me was Ron Jones, the man who would later marry Sally's sister Colleen. Occasionally, at mealtime I went to the cafeteria, took a used plate from a friend, and made a trip through the serving line to get "seconds."

As the year wore on, my shoulder continued to deteriorate and often popped out of place from simply sneezing. Once I nearly drowned when it popped out while I was swimming. Finally, I gave in and rode to Spokane to see a doctor. While I was in town I saw Sally by chance near the office where she worked. We struck up a conversation and subsequently rekindled our relationship. A few months later, I scraped together enough money to pay for shoulder surgery. Sally was the only person who visited me while I recovered. As my shoulder healed, our relationship grew and friendship turned to romance.

In the summer of 1961, Sally and I were married at St. Joseph's Catholic Church in Sandpoint, Idaho. The Rev. John Dahlberg officiated. Our parents attended the ceremony, along with Sally's sisters and brothers. After a short honeymoon trip, we settled in an apartment and I returned to my job—grueling work in a pole yard where we turned trees from the nearby forests into telephone poles. A few weeks later, I learned that Idaho regulations allowed me to teach even though I hadn't completed my bachelor's degree. I applied to the school board for a position and was accepted for a job teaching seventh grade at Southside Elementary School in Cocolalla, a small town not far from Sandpoint. It didn't pay much more than the job at the pole yard, but it was a teaching position and the hours gave me more time to hunt and fish. By then hunting and fishing were as much a part of my life as eating and sleeping. In between teaching and hunting I supplemented our income by waiting tables at the Elks Club.

Early the following year, our son, Chuck Jr., was born. In what had become my typical fashion, I paid the hospital bill with a jar full of quarters. The following year, our daughter Heather was born and I moved up to teach ninth-grade science at Sandpoint Junior High. I also coached football, basketball, and track. That summer I completed the requirements for my bachelor's degree and returned to Eastern Washington for graduation. But with a growing family, money was tight and I couldn't afford the fifteen-dollar graduation robe. Instead of attending and receiving my degree with my classmates, I watched the ceremony through a hole in the fence.

In February 1964, Sarah was born. Sally had been restless the night before, so when she awoke with labor pains, we were not surprised. I helped her into the car and started toward the hospital. It wasn't far from our house. On the way, we passed the local car dealership, Sandpoint Motors. The building was on fire and I stopped to watch the owner drive the cars from the showroom.

The scene was entertaining for me—flames in the air and people running around in a hurry to get the cars out. Sally was already in labor and as you might imagine, she didn't think it was entertaining at all. By then the labor pains were severe and rapid. She wasn't much interested in watching the fire or anything else. We made it to the hospital in time and Sarah was delivered by Dr. Helen Peterson.

Helen was a graduate of Sandpoint High School. She obtained an undergraduate degree from the University of Idaho, then studied medicine at Case Western Reserve. She returned to Sandpoint in 1946 as the town's first female doctor and practiced there until the 1950s when she contracted tuberculosis. Her office was closed for a couple of years while she fought to overcome the illness. Eventually, she recovered and picked up her medical practice once more.

I think about that sometimes—the town's first female doctor delivering Alaska's first female governor, who became the first female candidate on the Republican Party's national ticket. They both rose from humble beginnings to become tenacious women who overcame many professional obstacles.

Everything I needed to know I learned on the basketball court.

Sarah Palin

CHAPTER 5

Sports

*Next to religion, sports was the most
important thing in our lives.*
CHUCK HEATH JR.

I n 1978, my junior year in high school, I was the starting tail-
back on the varsity football team at Wasilla High School. One
weekend we traveled down to Anchorage to take on the team from
Anchorage Christian School. At the beginning of the game we
didn't play very well and they ran us up and down the field for the
first two quarters. At halftime we were behind by a score of 26–0.

The stadium where we played had no locker rooms, so during the break we loaded onto the school bus to rest and try to
regroup. Coach Olson yelled and shouted at us with one of those
"Where's your character?" halftime speeches. He recounted for
us in excruciating detail how poorly we'd performed and blasted
us for letting down our families, our school, and most important,
ourselves.

When play resumed in the third quarter we were more than
ready to turn things around. Our second-half effort was some of
the best football we played all year. Mike Koeneman, our quarter-
back, threw four touchdown passes and I ran for 181 yards. The
defense played well and held Anchorage Christian to a scoreless

second half. We put up thirty unanswered points and won the game, 30–26.

After the game, parents and friends came by to congratulate us. Sarah sauntered over to where I was standing and looked at me. "You know, Chuck," she began, "I used to tell people you weren't my brother until you started doing so well on the football field." It was the kind of comment one might expect from a younger sister who was still just a freshman in high school, but it summed up the value we placed on sports. Next to religion, sports was the most important thing in our lives—and it still is, even though it now takes a heavier toll on our bodies.

Last year, while playing in a men's hockey league, I collided with a friend, Andrew Friesen. We were skating toward each other at full speed and his shoulder struck me squarely in the sternum. The force of the collision sent us sprawling onto the ice, where we lay stunned and in pain. After the game, I noticed my heart rate seemed erratic—fast one moment and slow the next. Before long, my jaw hurt, my shoulder throbbed, and pain stabbed me in the chest. An hour later I was at the hospital emergency room, but when trauma physicians examined me they couldn't find anything wrong. As a precaution, they drew a blood sample and sent it to the lab, where they discovered I had an elevated troponin level, an indication my heart muscle had sustained damage. Further tests by my cardiologist, Mario Binder, revealed I was suffering from a near-fatal torn coronary artery. Some would suggest that I'm too old for that kind of sport and they're probably correct, but sports are a big part of me and a lifestyle I am passing on to my children. At the time of my injury, my eleven-year-old son, Kier, and I were training for a climb up Mount McKinley that would make him the youngest person to reach the summit. We've been living this way our entire lives and I doubt there's much chance we'll quit anytime soon.

As you might expect, we began playing organized sports at an early age. I started with baseball. Heather, Sarah, and Molly began organized sports with the Little Dribblers program, a basketball league that focused on children in the elementary grades. It's a national program with teams and leagues all over the country. The league in Wasilla was organized by Reid Smith. He'd come to Anchorage to work with his brothers in the insurance adjusting business. Their offices were located in the city but rather than live amid the urban congestion, Reid and his family bought a house in Wasilla.

Reid had been a successful high school coach in Texas. The move to Alaska was supposed to represent a break from that career, yet when he noticed that the Mat-Su Valley lacked organized sports for children he couldn't ignore it, and he set about filling the void. Dad and Mom signed all of us up as soon as the league was formed. That first summer we had more than twenty teams and Reid ended up coaching more in Alaska as a volunteer than he did in Texas where it was part of his job.

Our parents played too, though not in the Little Dribblers league. The men met on Wednesday nights and played basketball in the school gym. Those games included Reid and Jay Smith, Ray Carter, Curt Menard, Rod Cottle, and Dad. They all were very competitive and played an aggressive brand of basketball, but as far as I know they kept it friendly. On Wednesdays, their wives joined them for coed volleyball. The volleyball games they played with the wives were sometimes more rambunctious than the all-male basketball games.

As we grew older, Sarah played softball in the summer. Reid Smith was the softball coach too. Our area of the state didn't have many girls' softball teams and the ones we did have weren't much competition for the Wasilla team. To fill out the schedule, Reid arranged games against women's teams from Anchorage. Reid remembered, "Some of those teams included college students. We didn't win too many of those games, but after playing them the high school teams in our area weren't much trouble." Tammy Smith Bunker, Reid's daughter and one of Sarah's teammates, remembered playing with Sarah on the team. "We played in the state tournament one year and came in second." The team also played in regional tournaments twice, once in Portland and then in Seattle.

During the academic year we participated in organized sports on school teams, first in junior high and then in high school. Sarah continued to enjoy playing softball and she ran on the track and cross-country teams. However, the sport she loved the most was basketball. She wasn't very tall and she wasn't really that good on offense, but she made up for it with hard work. She also was smart. When asked about it, one of her coaches, Cordell Randall, said, "She learned quickly that the key to the game was getting the ball to Heidi and Wanda, our tallest players. She got very good at working the ball inside."

Much has been written about Sarah's role as a leader on the girls' basketball team and about how others on the team wanted to play well so they wouldn't let her down. In reality, the mold for that team was cast years before Sarah and her classmates took the court.

When we moved to Wasilla, the town had one gas station and one small store operated by the Teeland family. The road from Anchorage was a gravel road and it ended not far from our house. For the most part, the kids who were active in extracurricular activities at school participated in all the school's activities. Those who played softball also ran track. The ones who played football often played on the basketball team too. And most of us spent a few years in the band. I played trombone. Heather, Sarah, and Molly played the flute. Everyone knew everyone. Our parents were good friends with the Carter and Erickson families, who had children approximately the same age as us. The three families played together, hunted together, camped together, and looked after one another.

Our sister Heather, arguably the best athlete in the family and by far the most competitive, entered girls' sports first. She brought with her a work ethic that had been ingrained in us from a very early age. That devotion to hard work translated into aggressive play on the basketball court and a determination to win. In her senior year, her girls' basketball team reached the finals of the state tournament, something that no other team in our school's history had ever accomplished. They came up short in the final game, but the example set by Heather and her teammates during their four years of high school play created a culture of work and discipline that was passed to succeeding classes.

Reporters have written about the tournament that year and how Don Teeguarden, the girls' head coach, and Cordell Randall, his assistant, went to breakfast the morning following the game thinking the team was still in their rooms, recovering from the loss the night before. As they emerged from the restaurant they saw Heather and her teammates coming up the street. Rather than sleeping in, as most would have expected, the girls had gotten up early and gone to church. A similar incident happened two years before on a trip to Cordova for a Saturday game. The following day, Sunday, on the ferry ride back home, most of the girls gathered in a quiet place on the boat and held their own worship service. Sarah was a sophomore that year. The service on the ferry was led by Heather and members of the senior class.

Two summers during Sarah's high school years, she attended

a sports camp in Texas that was conducted by Davy Hobson. She went there with several kids from our area, including Darin Swift, the son of an oil-field employee who came to Alaska as the pipeline neared completion. Reid Smith arranged for Sarah and the others to participate in the program as a way of giving the girls her age an opportunity to expand their playing experience. On the way to that program, they spent the night at the home of Reid's in-laws. While there, the girls attended a Sunday worship service at the local church. Everyone noticed that Sarah and the other girls all had their Bibles with them. "That might not have been important to anyone else," Reid remembered, "but to us it was a big deal." Sarah took her faith seriously, even at a young age.

Team leadership didn't just apply to worship on Sundays or play on the court. The girls of that era treated academic studies with the same serious approach. In order to play, they had to maintain good grades. Many of their games required overnight travel, which meant they sometimes missed classes and often were gone for the weekend. The absences from school didn't count against them, but they still had to complete the coursework. Most people on the team brought their books with them on the trip and studied on the bus. No one made them do it. They did it on their own. Heather and her teammates, beginning in their freshman year, were particularly diligent and set an example that was passed from class to class, spanning a ten-year period that included the class of Molly, our youngest sister.

Molly was a good gymnast and a dominant basketball player. I remember watching her youth league basketball games and marveling at how she performed. She was the shortest girl on her team, but she was aggressive and never afraid to shoot. Her high school team didn't win the state championship, but her individual play caught the eye of coaches from across the state. In her senior year she was selected for membership on the Alaska High School Basketball Association's All-Star Team and played in that year's showcase game, an honor none of the rest of us ever received.

As good as she was at basketball Molly also was a successful sprinter. When she was in the fourth grade she competed in the Jesse Owens Games, where she won the state championship in the 4 x 100 relay. That effort earned her a trip to Los Angeles, where she competed against teams from across the nation. At the opening ceremony she watched in awe as Wilma Rudolph, America's first international women's track star and a three-time Olympic gold medalist, carried the torch into the stadium. In the ninth grade, Molly again qualified for the Jesse Owens Games and returned to Los Angeles. This time, she had the honor of carrying the torch for the opening ceremony. We still have pictures of Jesse Owens placing a gold medal around her neck at the conclusion of the games.

During her first three years of high school, Sarah watched most of her basketball games from a seat on the bench. Heather, a year ahead of her, was a starter on the team and the other positions were filled with talented, experienced players. Reid Smith remembered, "Those girls could read each other's minds, particularly Heather and Tammy." Most games, Sarah had to sit and watch as the older girls took the floor. In her junior year she began politicking with Coach Randall about getting more varsity game time. "You've got to get me in there," she kept telling him. "You have to get me in the game." He got her in the game, but not the one she wanted.

As an assistant coach, Randall had full responsibility for the junior varsity team. He convinced Coach Teeguarden that playing Sarah on the junior varsity team would be good for her. She didn't like it, and did more than her share of complaining, but once her feet hit the court she gave it her all. "Her face used to get red when she played," Randall remembered. "I used to wonder if it was red because she was working hard, or if she was just mad at me." Regardless of how she felt about it, the team won almost all their games and she obtained valuable playing experience.

In Sarah's senior year everyone thought the team would play well, but no one expected them to get very far in the state tournament. The year before when Heather was a senior and playing on the team, they made it to the finals, but most people thought that was a fluke. Wasilla High School wasn't very large, and to win the championship they had to compete against much larger schools from Anchorage. With a larger student body from which to draw players, those city schools fielded squads that were usually far more talented and experienced than any of the smaller, more rural schools.

That year, Sarah started as point guard. Surrounded by a group of hardworking teammates, they played well throughout the schedule. Sarah's greatest contribution was on defense, where her aggressive style of play more than made up for her lack of size and shooting ability. She simply outhustled her opponents and wore them down. She had always been stubborn, and on the basketball court she turned that stubbornness into tenacity. Regardless of whom she was assigned to guard, she just never gave up.

In their final game of the regular season Sarah's team faced East Anchorage High School, arguably the best team in the state. Wasilla's group of overachievers was no match for the city school and went down in a bitter and humiliating defeat. Undaunted, they set about preparing for the state tournament the same way they had prepared for every other game that year—they went to work. In the first round of the tournament they drew a rematch with East Anchorage. Everyone in town thought Wasilla's tournament play would be over before it began.

When Sarah and her team arrived for that first game, many of the best players for East Anchorage sat out the pregame warm-ups, choosing to relax in the stands and watch. "When I saw that," Randall recalled, "I knew we had a chance."

A few weeks earlier, during the final game of the season, Sarah twisted her ankle. Later we learned she'd suffered a hairline fracture, but nothing would keep her from playing in the tournament. She didn't get as much time on the court during the tournament as she did during the regular season, but her effort on defense helped contain East Anchorage's offense.

The opening game of the tournament turned out to be the championship game, and when East Anchorage went down to defeat, Coach Teeguarden and Coach Randall turned their attention to keeping the team focused on the next game. On paper, all the teams in the remaining rounds were inferior to Wasilla. Teeguarden didn't want Sarah and her teammates to get surprised, just as they had surprised East Anchorage. They needn't have been concerned. The team approached each game with the same workmanlike attitude they'd displayed all year and methodically advanced from round to round. The whole town was proud when they won the final game.

Sarah has said many times that playing on that team and in that tournament was one of the biggest events of her life. She is often quoted as saying, "Everything I needed to know I learned on the basketball court." That's a bit of an overstatement, but playing basketball was important because for the first time in her life she understood what Dad and Mom had been telling us: "If you work hard and do your best, things will turn out right." Playing basketball showed her that what they'd been saying was true and provided a tangible result she not only could see but feel as well.

Coach Teeguarden once said, "Sarah was well on her way to being Sarah long before she picked up a basketball." That's true, but playing on that team was an eye-opening experience for her and a turning point in the development of her character. It was a major time of transition, when a child's insistence on having her own way grew into the resolve of an adult shaping the outcome of her life through her own effort. Our friend Kim Ketchum said, "Sarah wasn't one of those people who let life happen. She saw what she wanted and made life happen." That part of Sarah's character came to the forefront as she played on the basketball team in her senior year.

Sarah and her teammates took play on the basketball court seriously and wanted others to take them seriously too. In Teeguarden's words, "They didn't want it to be treated like intramurals." He also noticed a growing edge to Sarah's personality. "She always had an opinion and was willing to share it with you in a respectful way, which is what we want kids to do."

Playing on that team gave her an opportunity to express herself with adults in the context of a collaborative relationship that went beyond the interaction she had with our parents and beyond merely the relationship of student to teacher. For one of the first times in her life, she was a participant with adults in a venture that was bigger than either of them. It was an experience she would encounter many times in the years that followed.

Later, in college, Sarah majored in journalism as a way of combining a lifelong interest in writing with an equal interest in sports. As part of her work toward that degree, she applied for an internship as a sports reporter at KTUU, a television station in Anchorage. I say she applied—actually she just showed up at the studio with a résumé and asked to see the person in charge of the sports department. John Hernandez, the sports director for the station, happened to be in the office that day and agreed to see her. He was impressed that she had the temerity to step out and take control of her life. "She saw what she wanted and was doing her best to make it happen." That assertive nature took her a step further when she won a seat on the city council.

In 1992, Sarah was a young mother. Track, her eldest son, was four years old. Since marrying Todd she'd become friends with the mayor of Wasilla, John Stein. She also was acquainted with Nick Carney, who was serving a term on the council. When Sarah expressed an interest in city government, Nick encouraged her to run for an open seat. Sarah campaigned hard and, with the help of friends and family, she won the election. Having supported her from the start, I think Nick assumed she would be his ally on the council. If she was, it wasn't for long. Things changed rather quickly.

One of the first issues the new council faced was a proposal to require all residents of Wasilla to pay for garbage pickup. Until then, everyone was free to dispose of their own garbage however they chose. Nick operated the town's only garbage service. Many people used his company, but no one was compelled to use it. Sarah saw the proposed ordinance as a conflict of interest—the city council passing an ordinance that in effect required all citizens to use a garbage service operated by a member of the council. Nick hadn't proposed the ordinance, and he abstained from voting on the issue, but that didn't solve the problem for Sarah. To her, it was simply a conflict of interest and one more intrusion of government on the lives of private citizens.

Instead of bowing to the obvious political pressure to "go along to get along," she voted against the measure. Not only that, she was quite vocal in her opposition. For Sarah, it was the only thing to do. In her mind, voting against the proposal was a choice between right and wrong. In the bigger picture, however, taking a stand on the issue, in direct opposition to the views of key people who helped her gain elected office, was a necessary step toward becoming a politician in her own right, rather than someone else's pawn.

If Nick, the mayor, and others in city government were surprised by Sarah's assertiveness, those of us who knew her well were not. We saw that trait first blossom years before on the high school basketball court.

We eat, therefore we hunt.

Sarah Palin

CHAPTER 6

Getting There

So, at the end of the school year in 1964, having never been
to Alaska and taking it sight unseen, I said good-bye to
Sandpoint, packed up the station wagon, and headed north.
CHUCK HEATH SR.

From the time I was ten years old I dreamed of living in the outdoors. As a child I read novels by Jack London and Laura Ingalls Wilder. Her Little House series appealed to my interest in living and surviving off the land. London's novels heightened my interest in Alaska. Idaho offered plenty of opportunities, but my father always said Alaska was the real hunter's paradise.

Three guys I met while in the Army stoked my interest, and reports about Alaskan statehood filled the newspapers in the early 1960s. Alaska had only been admitted to the Union in 1959. My childhood friend Ray Carter, also a teacher, and his wife, Kris, caught the Alaska bug too. In 1963, they moved up there, attracted by the lure of life in the new frontier and the prospect of higher pay. At the time, Idaho teachers' salaries were the lowest in the nation. Alaska's were the highest. The Carters taught in Huslia, a native Alaskan town sixty miles south of the Arctic Circle. With Ray and Kris gone, it seemed time was passing me by.

Three of our children, Chuck Jr., Heather, and Sarah, were

born in Sandpoint, and I had grown up there. The region had many things to offer, and I knew almost everyone in the area. Our family was expanding and the children, though still quite young, were getting older. Life had fallen into a comfortable routine. Still, the prospect of adventure in Alaska tugged at my soul and I knew if we were ever going to leave, we'd have to go soon. I told Sally we would go for a year and give it a try. That was really just a cover story for her parents. They thought we were crazy. Sally weighed the consequences for our family but she never seriously opposed the move. Asked about it later she said, "It sounded like a fun thing to do." She knew we weren't coming back.

While I continued to teach at Sandpoint, I filed applications with several school districts in Alaska. Most of those applications were rejected. I found out later they turned me down because we had small children. Most of the teaching vacancies were in remote villages. They were concerned we wouldn't last long in the bush with kids that young.

Later in the year I finally received two offers. One was from a remote village. I guess they were desperate for teachers. The other was from a school in Skagway. I chose Skagway because it had a hospital. With three young children, having a hospital nearby seemed like a good idea. We didn't find out until later that the "hospital" really was a clinic without a regular full-time doctor.

At the end of the school year in 1964, having never been to Alaska and taking it sight unseen, I said good-bye to Sandpoint, packed up the station wagon, and headed north. From Idaho, I drove to Prince Rupert, British Columbia, then put the car on a ferry for the last leg of the trip into Skagway. Sally and the children came later that summer, after I got settled.

The town of Skagway is located north of Juneau at the head of the Taiya Inlet, the extreme northern end of the Inside Passage, once a favored route for ships seeking to avoid the dangers of plying the open waters of the northern Pacific. Situated in the panhandle of southeastern Alaska, it lies in the southern portion of the state, that tiny finger of land that runs alongside the Canadian province of British Columbia. Its name is derived from the Tlingit Indian word *skagua*, meaning "a windy place with white caps on the water." As anyone who has lived there will tell you, the name is well deserved.

In 1887, a former steamboat captain named William Moore had claimed a homestead at the mouth of the Skagway River. He had become familiar with the area while working on a survey crew mapping the Klondike region. The area was geologically similar to regions in California, Mexico, and South America, where gold had been discovered. Moore believed the Klondike was rich with the ore too. He built a sawmill and a wharf at the head of Taiya Inlet in anticipation of what he was certain would be a rush of miners into soon-to-be-discovered goldfields. Nine years later, a prospector proved him right. The following year, the first of many steamers docked at Moore's Wharf.

By 1898, Skagway's population approached ten thousand people, which made it the largest city in the Alaska Territory. With this sudden growth came the typical problems that most mining boomtowns experienced. Old-timers used to say it was more profitable to "mine the miners" than to actually mine a claim. To hear them tell it, the town had about as many crooks and swindlers as it had honest, hardworking people. When we arrived, there were still people who remembered the old days and the town retained much of its gold-rush character.

One of the most notorious criminals was a man named Jefferson Randolph "Soapy" Smith. A con man and a swindler, he came to Skagway in 1898 and established a telegraph office. He charged an exorbitant fee to miners trying to wire messages to their loved ones down south. Unbeknownst to them, telegraph wires in Soapy's office went no farther than the wall. He enjoyed the high life from that and other swindles until citizens of the town grew tired of his antics. He was shot and killed on the Juneau Wharf. We visited his gravesite, which wasn't far from our house.

When we arrived in Skagway, the old wooden sidewalks, a necessity years earlier for keeping foot traffic out of the muddy, unpaved streets, were still in use. Many of them had been there since the town was originally established. Not long after we arrived, the city tore them out. We joined others who searched the ground beneath the sidewalks and found a number of silver coins and other memorabilia from the gold-rush days.

In the 1960s, oil exploration was the new gold rush. As in the past, people flocked to Alaska to seek their fortune, only now the prospectors were large multinational corporations. Individuals came for high-paying jobs working the rigs. Skagway didn't participate much in the oil rush, but it did participate in the tourist rush as cruise ships brought more and more sightseers to view the Alaskan coastline.

Our first two homes in Skagway were located in an area known as the Tank Farm—a fuel depot constructed during World War II to supply the soldiers who were building the Alaskan Highway. In addition to attacking Pearl Harbor, Japan occupied some of the Aleutian Islands as part of their strategy to control trade routes across the northern Pacific. The Alaskan Highway was designed to connect Alaska with the lower forty-eight states as part of the Allied defense against a potential invasion. The Tank Farm was located at the northern end of town, just off what is now the Klondike Highway.

Houses at the Tank Farm were simple and cheap. We lived in

a duplex first, then moved to a single-family dwelling. Later we lived closer to town in a house originally owned by Edward Rasmuson. His son, Elmer, would later become president of the Bank of Alaska, mayor of Anchorage, and one of the wealthiest men in the state. Living in his house didn't make us any richer, but living in Alaska enriched our lives beyond measure.

During the academic year—fall through spring—I taught classes at the public school. In the summer, I worked on the White Pass and Yukon Railroad, building bridges and maintaining the rail line up the White Pass into the Yukon Territory. At night I tended bar at the Igloo, a local drinking establishment. I also found time to drive a taxi. With five of us to feed, I took every job I could find. Sally stayed busy too, looking after our children and keeping things running smoothly at home. She also contributed financially by working at a jewelry store, driving a taxi, and helping at the museum during tourist season.

Despite a full schedule, I never forgot why I came to Alaska and squeezed in hunting or fishing trips whenever possible. Because of Skagway's proximity to the ocean, trips to find moose and deer were often to hunting sites far from town. Unlike at my childhood home in Hope, I couldn't shoot big game out the window of my bedroom in Skagway. They weren't there. That was something I didn't realize until we moved. Sally and the children sometimes accompanied me, but usually they just greeted me when I returned home and helped wrap up the meat for the freezer. Hunting and fishing provided most of the protein in our diet.

One animal we could hunt close to home was seal. Seal hunting was still legal then and became an important source of income for us. At the time, sealskins sold for twenty-five dollars each. On a good day I could bring home three or four hides.

Life in Skagway followed a routine pattern. Routine for us, that is—work, home, hunting, fishing—but adventure was never far away. One day not long after we moved there, Sally was driving toward town in her Volkswagen microbus when she saw a man standing by the road waving his arms to flag her down. She stopped to help and learned he was an engineer from the railroad. He'd been spotting cars on a siding and somewhere in the process of unhooking the cars he'd stepped from the locomotive without properly setting the controls. When he turned around to reboard it, the locomotive was gone. Sally gave him a ride into town and caught up with the train as it rolled onto the wharf. The engineer bailed from the van and scrambled aboard the locomotive as it rumbled down the track toward the ocean. He managed to get it stopped just short of the end of the dock.

Two years after we moved to Skagway, Sally gave birth to Molly, our youngest daughter. As I mentioned earlier, I had chosen Skagway because it had a hospital, and I assumed that meant they had a resident doctor there as well. We found out later the doctor traveled between towns in the region and only came to the hospital at appointed times. Most people in need of medical care received it from a nurse. When Sally went into labor I drove her down to the hospital. Thankfully, the doctor was in town. I was at Sally's side when she gave birth.

Often when I tell about the event my account sounds as if I delivered the baby and the doctor assisted. That's how it felt at the time but I really didn't help that much. Sally did all the work. The doctor and I just stood by and watched. A few hours after the delivery, he sent us all home—me, Sally, and our newborn, Molly.

In 1969, Sally decided she'd had enough of life in Skagway and wanted to live in a less remote area. Back then, Skagway wasn't connected to the state highway system. She had seen a picture in the newspaper of children swimming in a lake in Anchorage and she decided our children should have the same opportunity. I enjoyed Skagway but wasn't opposed to the move. Living near Anchorage would give me access to the University of Alaska, where I could obtain a master's degree. Having an advanced degree would increase my pay and the opportunity for advancement as a teacher.

To make the move I needed a teaching job. Through that summer I applied for several positions and went on a number of interviews, but from the less-than-enthusiastic reception I received, and with teaching jobs already scarce, I felt there was little chance of landing a position. Then one night while hanging out at the Igloo, I heard a familiar voice in the crowd. It turned out to be the voice of Russ Kramer, brother to my high school teammate Jerry. He asked what I was doing and I caught him up on the news of our move from Idaho. Then I explained our desire to relocate to Anchorage and the tough time I was having finding a job. Russ listened attentively, then grinned and said, "I live in Anchorage. The assistant superintendent of the school system is my neighbor." He picked up the phone in the bar and placed a call. A few days later, I had a job teaching in the Anchorage district.

We lived in Russ's basement for a few weeks, then moved to an apartment in a town called Eagle River, which is about fifteen miles north of Anchorage. We spent two years there but between teaching, attending class at the university, and hunting, I didn't see much of my family.

In 1971, while I was out of town guiding sheep hunters through the Wrangell Mountains, Sally found a house that was for sale in Wasilla. Not many houses were available then and she thought it was a great deal. I was in the bush and she had no way to communicate with me. So she made an offer on the property by herself. Buying that house turned out to be one of the best investments we ever made.

To people living in Anchorage, Wasilla was a hick town. Our children didn't think of it that way, but they had become attached to each of the places we lived—first Skagway, then Anchorage, then Eagle River. Each time we moved they missed their old friends and spent time reminiscing about how great life was where we used to live and how tough it was in the new place. They complained about making yet one more move, but living in Wasilla turned out to be great for us.

Our new house was nice but small. For the first couple of years, all four children shared the same bedroom. In an effort to maintain a bit of personal space, they divided the small room into quarters using masking tape on the floor. No one was allowed to cross the other's line without an invitation. As you can imagine, living in such confined quarters led to more than a few fights. Not long before I retired we sold the house and built a new one farther out from town. Our old house became the Mocha Moose Coffee Shop. You can tour it now with a cup of coffee and see where we used to live.

In the summer the kids spent time at the swimming hole at Wasilla Lake. Nowadays, people take their children for lessons to teach them to swim. Back then, we told them to jump in and figure it out for themselves. When they weren't swimming in the lake, they were at the school playing baseball or in the backyard where they had a dirt basketball court. We had a television, but I put it in storage during the summer. In our part of Alaska, the sun sets for only four hours in the summer and the mountains were never far away. There was too much to see and do to spend time in front of the television.

Between June and September, we used to ride out to Knik Road near Wasilla and hike down to the mouth of Cottonwood Creek, where we fished for salmon. The creek drains into the Knik Arm of Cook Inlet. Spring and summer salmon runs brought the fish up the creek to spawn. To get to the best spot, we had to walk along a bluff that overlooked the inlet. Sarah, Heather, and Chuck Jr. went with me many times. On several occasions I led them through a grove of birch trees that hid the remains of dwellings once occupied by the Dena'ina people.

The Dena'ina people were part of the Athabascan aboriginal group that inhabited most of southeastern Alaska long before Europeans arrived. Their region stretched from Seldovia on the Kenai Peninsula, west as far as Lime Village, and north of Wasilla to Chickaloon. Prior to the arrival of Russian explorers, they lived along both sides of the Cook Inlet, from the mouth of the Knik River all the way to the ocean. Back then, they migrated from hunting camps north of the inlet to fishing camps near the water.

As Europeans settled around present-day Anchorage and gradually moved up the inlet, the Dena'ina retreated to the upper reaches of Knik Arm. Disease and disruptions to their traditional hunting and fishing patterns took a heavy toll on them but they remained an organized group in the area well into the twentieth century. Many were assimilated into the local culture. Today, there are only about 1,400 Dena'ina in the area. Some, primarily those who live in and around Lime Village, work hard to preserve the Dena'ina language and traditional lifestyle. Raymond Theodore, a descendant of the original Dena'ina, was one of Chuck Jr.'s childhood friends.

The site on the bluff is protected now but when our children were young they used to stand in the sunken foundations of the dwellings above the creek and imagine what it was like to live there hundreds of years ago. Our area has continued to develop, but you can still look in a particular direction without seeing man-made objects. With that unobstructed view, it's easy to let your mind wander back to imagine the kind of life the Dena'ina might have lived. I find it amazing that traces of the past, a time that existed so long ago, can still be visible today.

When our children were younger, we spent a lot of time with Ray Carter and his family, camping, hunting, and fishing together. Ray wasn't much of a hunter but he loved to camp and bought an old yellow school bus that he converted into a motor home. It didn't look like much but it had bunk beds and a kitchen. There were eight kids—our four along with Marie, Thor, Chad, and Amy Carter—plus the four adults, which made for a crowd, even in a school bus. Rich and Julie Erickson joined us sometimes and brought their children—Chrissie, Richie, and Deanna. With seventeen people in the bus, I suspect we looked like a group of hippies on the way to a commune, but we had a great time on those trips. We took the bus up to Denali Park a number of times and on camping trips into the bush.

Between seasons, when the weather was warm, we took the children fossil hunting. I located several privately owned tracts where I'd noticed a number of promising rock formations—it's illegal to take prehistoric artifacts from state or federal land—and we often turned the trips into a weekend of camping. During the daylight hours we tramped through the woods and waded along the banks of creeks and rivers in search of items preserved from a time thousands of years ago when humans first entered the Alaska region. We found many examples of fossilized alder, oak, and sequoia leaves, and also sections of petrified wood. On a couple of trips we located perfectly preserved mammoth teeth and pieces of mammoth-tusk ivory, too. Mammoths disappeared from the continental mainland about eight to ten thousand years ago. To hold something in our hands from that ancient time set our imaginations alive with images of a wilderness untouched by humans.

On later trips we expanded our collection with fossilized bones from prehistoric bison, caribou, and horses. My favorite find was a steppe bison skull. Steppe bison became extinct about the same time as the mammoths. Almost as intriguing were the marine specimens of ammonites, clams, and scallops. Their natural habitat would have placed them at the bottom of the ocean, yet we found them at elevations above eight thousand feet.

Today, our children use many of those pieces as decorations in their own homes. I have a sizeable number in my basement and continue to search for new specimens with our grandchildren. When Sarah and Todd built their home, we selected about forty fossils from our collection and embedded them in their fireplace and along the hearth.

In the winter, when everything was covered with snow and all the lakes were frozen, we went ice-fishing. Most of our fishing was done on Lake Lucille, the same lake where Sarah lives today. Not many people ice-fished then, which meant fish were plentiful. So much so that the only thing needed for bait was a piece of neon yarn. Cheetos worked too, if you could get them to stay on the hook. Fish eggs were the best but we had to thaw them out to put them on the hook. That required holding the frozen lump in your mouth until it became soft enough to attach it to the line. Our daughters balked at doing that.

Lake Lucille was also our favorite duck hunting spot, which is hard to believe now because the shore is lined with houses. Every fall, we'd canoe across the lake to a marshy area and lay our decoys, then sit back and wait for the ducks to arrive. One time, when Chuck Jr. was about eleven, a flock of ducks swooped in to land with our decoys. He got excited and began shooting way too soon. He missed the ducks but managed to sink three decoys. I fished one of them out of the water and mounted it on a plaque, which I hung with our other trophies in the living room.

On another occasion, Sarah and I paddled the canoe around the point near that same location just as Chuck Jr. took a shot at a duck. Pellets from his shotgun peppered the canoe. Sarah didn't like it and even though I explained to her that, as long as she protects her eyes, falling pellets from a shotgun wouldn't injure her, she was still upset by the incident. I shouted at Chuck Jr., mostly so he wouldn't shoot again. He heard the tone of my voice, threw down the gun, and ran for home. It sounds funny now. I'm not sure we laughed about it back then.

That same year I took Chuck Jr. to the Wrangell Mountains on his first sheep hunt. We flew into the bush and landed on a glacial lake, then hiked to our first camp, which was about twenty miles away. By the end of the day, he was groaning and complaining but he didn't quit.

The following year, while stalking a couple of rams, we climbed up the face of the mountain trying to reach the plateau where the animals stood. He went up the steep side. I took the gentler approach. A few minutes later I heard him call to me. From the sound of his voice I knew he was in trouble and when I looked in his direction I saw why. He had reached a spot where the rock face leaned out over his head. To continue upward, he would have to climb with his hands and allow his feet to dangle free. That wasn't possible. He was several hundred feet up the mountain carrying a heavy backpack with a rifle strapped over his shoulder. Trapped in no-man's land, he couldn't go up and he couldn't go down.

I worked my way toward him but I was still fifteen feet away. By then I could see the adrenaline had kicked in and Chuck Jr.

was near panic. Coaching him down wasn't going to work. I did my best to remain calm but I was worried. One slip and he would drop all the way to the bottom.

While I continued to talk to him, trying to ease the tension of the moment, I noticed a ledge just a few feet below. He could have backed his way to it, but being unable to see his feet, he couldn't find the toeholds to do it. Finally, I reached behind my back and worked my fingers into a pocket on my backpack, where I found a nylon rope. I wrapped one end around my wrist and threw the other end to Chuck Jr. "Catch it," I said, "and I'll lower you to the ledge."

"No," he replied, shaking his head. "I can't get it. If I miss, I'll fall."

"You won't miss."

"Yes, I might."

"There's no other way."

This conversation went back and forth until I convinced him he had no choice. The next time the rope swung in his direction, he lunged for it and grabbed it with both hands. His body swung around backward and banged the rifle against the rocks, but he held on and I lowered him to the ledge. The rifle was scuffed and scraped but I was just grateful we made it out alive.

My hunting experiences with Sarah weren't quite that life-threatening, but she did give us all a scare once. When the children were young we spent a lot of time in the mountains, camping, hiking, and stalking animals. Some of our favorite things to stalk were Dall sheep. Through trial and error we learned that if we dressed in white, and came toward them with the wind in our face so they couldn't smell us, we could slip within twenty or thirty feet of them before their keen eyesight picked us up. Approaching them that way, we were able to observe them at close range.

We saw sheep giving birth to their lambs and watched those young lambs hide beneath their mothers' bellies to avoid being taken by an eagle. Lying quietly on the ground, we saw wolves attack and chase the herd—neither sheep nor wolf aware that we were just a few yards away. Once we watched two rams fighting. Again and again they charged toward each other, rising up on their back legs, then slamming their foreheads together with a force that staggered them both. It made a terrible racket and sounded as if the collision would smash their skulls. Rams have a honeycombed skull but rather than being filled with air like most animals, theirs is filled with a liquid that helps absorb the shock of the collision. However, that day, after the rams fought for a while, they paused, walked over to a snowbank, and buried their heads in the snow. I guess it hurt more than zoologists might imagine.

When Sarah was seven or eight years old, we were up in the mountains stalking sheep. She was dressed in white with sweatpants and a hooded sweatshirt. We crept up close to the sheep and lay on our bellies, watching them. After a while we moved to a different spot, then another. Then we noticed Sarah wasn't with us. For two hours we searched the mountainside, calling and shouting her name. I'd spent much of my life in the mountains and knew my way around the wilderness, but that day I was worried that something had happened to her. When we finally found her, she was stretched out on the ground near a snowbank, head resting on her arms, sound asleep. Dressed in white, she looked like a lump of snow and we'd probably walked right past her.

Many stories have been written about Sarah and her exploits as a hunter. She enjoys hunting even today, but does most of it now with Todd. When she was younger we spent much of our time together going after grouse, ptarmigan, rabbits, and caribou.

Several years ago we were hunting near the Denali Highway when I spotted several caribou standing about three hundred yards away. I pointed them out to Sarah and she got ready to shoot. Using my .225 caliber rifle, she lay on the ground, propped her arms on her elbows, and carefully sighted on the unsuspecting caribou. With a single shot, the animal slumped to the ground. A three-hundred-yard shot is difficult to make but she did it with ease on the first try.

A couple of years later we were in the same general area again. This time, Kevin Smith, a friend of ours, was with us. We spotted a caribou near our camp. It was quite a distance away but Sarah got into position to take a shot. "Aim above its back," I suggested. "At that distance, the bullet will drop a good bit." Sarah lay on the ground in prone position, steadied the rifle with her elbows, and squeezed off a shot. Once again, she dropped it on the first try. While we were watching, two more caribou stepped into view and Kevin got in position to shoot. He missed the first two times and didn't hit the animal until his third shot. Sarah is still good with a rifle, an ability she learned shooting birds with me and one she perfected as an adult on much larger game.

Our children remember their childhood as a time when we didn't have much money. It's true, feeding six of us meant money was tight, but we had a freezer full of game and Sally was a wonderful cook. Even our most discriminating guests rarely noticed the meat in the spaghetti sauce was moose, not beef. We didn't go hungry but we didn't eat out much either. I think we ate at a restaurant once while they were in high school.

We shopped a lot at thrift stores and once a year Sally ordered shoes and a few clothes from the Sears catalog. Our children were excited when the package finally arrived. I think they thought we did that because it was cheaper. The real reason was that Wasilla had no clothing stores. Shopping meant driving into Anchorage, which was a hundred-mile round-trip. Today we have a paved highway and the trip takes about an hour in each direction. Back then, the drive to Anchorage followed a winding narrow road. A shopping trip took an entire day.

Winter in Wasilla can be brutal. High winds roar down the valley from the Knik and Matanuska glaciers and funnel right through town. One winter, the wind blew so hard it tore the roofs off of houses and other buildings. Airplanes parked along the runway near our home were tossed around like toys. Snowdrifts piled up to the eaves. Still, we rarely let the extreme weather slow us down. If you are dressed for it, it can be a lot of fun.

In 1974, Sally's sister Colleen and brother-in-law Ron took the children to Expo 74, a world's fair event held in Spokane, Washington. The fair ran from May to November. They stayed at a hotel in Spokane that had an outdoor swimming pool. Greg Jones, Sally's nephew, remembered there was snow on the ground and ice crystals clung to the edge of the pool. Greg was huddled near a picnic table wearing his coat and trying to stay warm. Our children, including Sarah, were dressed in their swimsuits, splashing around in the pool with a beach ball. Once you get used to the cold temperatures in Alaska, the weather in other places doesn't seem extreme.

Even today, people outside of Alaska know little about what goes on in our state. I'm sure some people think Alaskans still live in igloos. That's not true—even in ancient times native Alaskans used igloos only as temporary shelter—but one winter our children and their friends cut blocks of snow from the drifts and built one in our yard. As I recall, it held thirteen kids and two dogs.

Most winters, our family spent the weekends at a place called Hatcher Pass, a cut through the Talkeetna Mountains, north of

Wasilla. Named for Robert Hatcher, a prospector who helped open the region for gold miners, the pass was only a half-hour drive from our house, but it was a lot different from Wasilla. It usually received much heavier snowfalls and was protected from the wind, which meant it was a great place to enjoy outdoor winter activities. The children learned to cross-country ski there and they learned to shoot ptarmigan, too. In the early years, Rufus, our German Shepherd, accompanied us. He was the only German Shepherd retriever I've ever known.

We need American energy brought
to you by American ingenuity and
produced by American workers.

Sarah Palin

CHAPTER 7

Work as a Lifestyle

*Beginning with junior high, when we weren't attending
school we were working.*
CHUCK HEATH JR.

For as long as I can remember, we had to work. As young children, our jobs included helping Mom clean house, maintaining the lawn, and cutting firewood. Our first house in Wasilla was heated with a wood-burning stove. Keeping warm in the cold Alaskan winter meant cutting wood in the summer. We burned lots of wood. Dressing wild game also was one of our chores. Animals we killed in the woods had to be skinned, butchered, and packaged for the freezer. Dad did the skinning and butchering. We did the rest. Heather and Sarah became particularly adept at the task.

Once, on an early-morning trip to Hatcher Pass, Dad killed a moose. It was a nice animal and we needed the meat, but time was short and he had to get back to town to teach class. He skinned and quartered the carcass, then gave Heather and Sarah the task of preparing the meat for the freezer. They worked on it the remainder of the day. When Dad returned that afternoon he found the skeleton picked clean. That might offend the suburban sensibilities of many Americans—most people today have no idea where their food comes from or the steps necessary to prepare it for consumption. We didn't have that luxury. Our meat came from the carcasses of animals we shot, killed, cleaned, and butchered. It was a process we learned at a young age.

As children, one of the ways we made extra money in the winter was by fur trapping. Since humans first arrived in Alaska, they have trapped animals, both for the meat and the hides. In many places, wearing animal skin for clothing has become unfashionable and politically incorrect. For Alaskan natives, skins were used to make traditional outerwear that was durable, waterproof, and warm. To the early Russian explorers, the fur trade was simply a means to an end.

From 1733 through 1744, Vitus Bering led an extensive Russian expedition from Siberia to map the Arctic Ocean. In 1741, one of his ships landed at Icy Bay near what is now the Alaskan border with Canada. A second ship went ashore a little farther south at Prince of Wales Island. Reports of what the explorers found brought more expeditions, most of them initially traveling only as far as the Aleutian Islands. There, the Russians discovered the fur trade. Rather than work the traps themselves, they enslaved the Aleuts to do it for them and began harvesting sea otters at an incredible pace. The Russians cared little for the native peoples and even less for the damage their harvesting practices inflicted on the region's ecology. As the otter population was depleted, the Aleuts were forced to hunt farther and farther from their homes. At the same time, the Russians pushed up the Aleutian Islands to the mainland, using brute force to subdue the Aleuts and financing their first settlements with profits from the fur trade. Though it is no longer the region's leading industry, trapping remains a significant business today.

Dad helped us set up a two-mile trapline along the Little

Susitna River. Twice each week we trudged through the snow to check our traps. Trapping is a lot like farming, except the harvest comes in winter. It involves hard work, too, and you don't get a day off because of bad weather or illness. Snowy or clear, well or ill, the traps had to be checked, baited, and reset. We were trapping mink. If the animals sat in the trap too long, shrews (small mouselike creatures) found them and attempted to eat them, rendering their fur useless.

In the Alaskan winter, there's not much daylight. It was always dark when we checked the trapline. Sometimes, depending on our schedule at school or with sports, we didn't get to the line until late at night. Dad would drop us off and we'd slip on our snowshoes, grab the flashlight, and head down the trail. The wind usually was blowing, which made the cottonwood trees creak and sent their shadows dancing across the snow. At night, as kids with just a flashlight for protection, we found it scary.

When we arrived home with the catch, we took the mink up to a small room on the second floor of our house. The room doubled as a reloading room—we loaded our own rifle shells from spent cartridges—and it was usually crowded with equipment and pelts from animals we'd previously caught. Dad skinned the mink and we stretched the pelts on boards so they could dry and cure. We never made a lot of money from trapping but we learned to work and value what little we made.

At the end of the sixth grade, I was twelve years old. The day after school ended, Dad asked me what I was doing that summer. I told him I wasn't sure. Probably playing baseball with my friends and swimming at the lake. "Wrong," he replied. "It's time for you to get a job. I want you to go door to door at every business in town until you find something. Do not come back to this house unless you've got a job."

The second door I knocked on was Crothers' Hardware Store. Ralph Crothers, the owner, moved to Wasilla in the 1950s. Everyone in town knew him. I was nervous about asking for work, but I knew Dad was serious about me getting a job. Not that he wanted me to help support the family. He didn't. He wanted me to learn the value of an income and the reward that comes with earning it. So, I mustered my courage and asked Ralph for a job. He wasn't interested in hiring anyone but I was persistent and offered to sweep the floors and clean up the lumberyard. He relented and told me I could work for one day and if I did a good job he'd consider adding me to his staff. I must have done all right because I ended up working five days a week all summer long.

From time to time my friends appeared at the fence behind the lumberyard and teased me about not getting to play baseball or swim in the lake. Of course, they all asked me for a loan after I started getting paid. Heather, Sarah, and Molly went through similar experiences. Beginning in junior high, whenever we weren't attending school we were working.

One summer, Heather and I worked in the Youth Conservation Corps helping build docks and nature trails near Anchorage. Sarah worked as a waitress at Farina's, a local fast-food place, and at the Roadside Café, about ten miles north of Wasilla. Molly worked at Archie's, a fast-food café on the Parks Highway, and spent a lot of time as a babysitter.

When Sarah began working at the Roadside Café, she didn't have her driver's license so someone had to drop her off and pick her up from work. After one of her shifts, I had to drive out and bring her home. I was aggravated about it but when I got out of the truck in the parking lot, I found a hundred-dollar bill on the ground. I had never seen a bill that large. I went into the restaurant and asked if anyone had lost any money. No one came forward, so I brought the money home. I kept it in a drawer for a few days because I was sure someone would come to claim it. No one ever did, so finally I put it in the bank. I never complained about picking up Sarah after work again.

As children, we didn't get many things handed to us. Mom and Dad provided for us—we didn't go hungry and we always had nice clothes to wear—but the extras in life were things we had to pay for ourselves. If we wanted a special jacket or something that wasn't merely necessary, we paid for it. When we wanted a particular piece of sports equipment, we had to find a way to buy it on our own. While Sarah was still in high school, she spent part of two summers at a sports camp in Texas. She traveled there with the Smiths and stayed at the home of Davy Hobson, who ran the sports program. The expenses weren't that much but she had to earn money to cover the cost. She also had to help the summer softball team raise money to cover the team's travel expenses. Reid Smith remembered, "Chuck and Sally didn't have much. Those kids had to earn their money." He was right. If we wanted it, we had to pay for it, and that meant finding work.

Hard work was good for us but I was envious of my friends who used their money to buy things they could enjoy like cars, trucks, and stereos. We never spent our money. Mom and Dad ingrained in us the notion that our savings was to be used only for college. The notion of delayed fulfillment, the ability to put off momentary pleasure today for an even bigger reward later, came to be an important concept in our lives.

When Sarah and Todd married, she was working as a sports reporter for the television station in Anchorage. She enjoyed the work but made very little money. Todd worked nights as a baggage handler at the airport. My sister Heather and I lived across the street from each other in West Anchorage. Many nights,

Sarah and Todd ended up crashing at Heather's after work instead of making the hour-long drive back to Wasilla.

Each evening at five o'clock, we gathered around the television to watch Sarah on the evening sports report. One of the people she interviewed was a female basketball player from the University of Alaska named Mitsy Swift. Mitsy was from George West, Texas. She and Sarah first met years earlier when Sarah and the group from Wasilla attended the sports camp hosted by Davy Hobson. Mitsy participated in that program, where she met Darin Swift, who'd come with the group from Alaska. Several years later, Darin and Mitsy married and returned to Anchorage, where Mitsy completed her last two years of college. "It was neat to see life come full circle like that," Darin remembered. "They played together as kids and then later Sarah interviewed her as a reporter."

Sarah took her job at the television station very seriously, but the five o'clock broadcast often was run with new, fresh-faced people behind the camera. There were a lot of technical glitches, such as Sarah introducing a video and the wrong one being shown. That drove her crazy. She worked hard to write a good report and expected others to work equally as hard to do their part.

Todd was born in Dillingham, a town that sits at the upper end of Bristol Bay, a large body of water on the west side of the Alaska Peninsula. Todd's father was born in Seattle, Washington, and worked in Alaska as a manager for the Matanuska Electric Association. His mother, however, was from a Yup'ik family that included members of the Curyung tribe. The Yupiit are an ancient people who migrated into Alaska from Siberia about ten thousand years ago. Todd's ancestors have fished the waters of Bristol Bay for thousands of years. As a young man, he followed in that tradition and from an early age worked on the family fishing skiffs. Factory ships operating in open waters off the coast provide much of the world's seafood products and reality television shows have glamorized the king crab business in the Bering Sea, but almost half the world's production of wild salmon comes from Bristol Bay.

Not long after Sarah and Todd married, Todd took a job working for an oil company on the North Slope. The work kept him away from home in two-week cycles. Two weeks on the slope, two weeks at home. Most years, he was able to arrange an extended time away from the job in order to continue working the summer fishing season. One year, however, he was unable to get time off. With commercial fishing providing a significant portion of their income, Sarah had no choice but to work the boat herself. Our father was recruited to help her. Many have written about Sarah's fishing experience and have raised questions about whether she actually participated. Dad saw firsthand how hard she worked.

Most commercial fishing in Bristol Bay is done with a set net—a gill net with a row of floats across the top and weights along the bottom. The floats keep the top edge of the net at the surface, while the weights force the net to hang vertically and keep the bottom edge several feet down in the water. One end of the net is anchored to the shore, then a crew working from a twenty-four-foot skiff drags the opposite end out into the bay. Once the net is in place, crews check it two or three times per hour. A crew member stands near the bow and pulls the net across the boat while others remove the fish. Fish taken from the net are placed into large bins that are lined with brailers—industrial-grade bags made of high-strength mesh that can hold up to a thousand pounds.

Salmon spend much of their life at sea, but in the spring and summer mature adult fish return to fresh water to spawn. They make that journey in large schools. As they come up the bay, the water becomes shallow and the fish are forced to remain near the surface, where they are caught in the net. Millions of sockeye, chinook, coho, and pink salmon follow this migratory pattern. Runs of fish moving up the bay are an amazing event.

Those runs come periodically through the summer fishing season and are the times when fishermen make their money. They also are the times when crews on the boats work the hardest. That summer, when Dad fished with Sarah, they worked one run that lasted for three days—that's three days and two nights without any sleep. It sounds impossible but working those runs is often the difference between making a profit for the season and not.

During one run that year, J. D. Palin, Todd's brother, took his boat out of the water. When Dad asked why, J. D. said he was going to a dance in Dillingham. Dad tried to convince him to stay and work his net but J. D. was determined to go to the dance. That night while he was gone, a run of salmon hit the bay. Sarah and Dad hauled in over ten thousand dollars' worth of fish. It happens just that fast.

Skiff boats work the bay night and day and no one wants to get off the water or go in to shore to unload, but fish can't lie in the boat long without spoiling. To facilitate the business and keep fishermen fishing, processing houses send larger boats out to purchase the catch. Those larger boats are called tenders. Some are huge and actually process the fish right there on the water. Most, however, are between sixty and a hundred feet long. Skiffs pull alongside the tender and crews on board use a boom and winch to haul the brailer bags onto the larger vessel, where the catch is weighed and recorded.

One night as they came alongside a tender, Sarah was in the stern working the motor to guide them close to the larger boat.

She had one hand on the control arm of the motor. The other rested on the gunwale of the skiff. The water wasn't particularly rough but the skiff bobbed and sloshed from side to side while they unloaded. One of the waves banged the skiff hard against the hull of the tender and smashed Sarah's hand between them. She howled and yelled in pain. Dad took a look at her hand and was sure she'd broken a couple of fingers. There was a clinic in Dillingham and he suggested they leave the net and go up there to have her hand checked. "No way," she replied. "We have to keep working." A few days later, when the salmon run subsided and they had time to visit the clinic, doctors found she'd broken three fingers.

At the end of the season, Sarah and Dad hauled in the net and took the boat ashore. Dad backed the truck and trailer down to the water, then manned the boat to run it onto the trailer. Three times he tried and each time he was unable to get the boat aligned properly. Finally, Sarah pushed him aside. "I'll do it," she insisted. She stepped into the boat and took hold of the control arm. Dad stood on the beach and watched the determined look in her eye as she gunned the engine and, in a single attempt, ran the boat all the way up onto the trailer.

When Sarah entered politics, that work ethic served her very well. In her first campaign, she and Todd didn't have much money to invest. On top of that, Sarah was uncomfortable asking for donations. She was accustomed to working for what she wanted. Several people did contribute to her campaign, but funds were always tight. Hard work made up the difference and became a characteristic of all her campaigns. In both mayoral elections and in the governor's race, work was the difference between winning and losing, a substitute for major donations. What others paid to accomplish, she and her supporters provided with the sweat of their brow in a truly grassroots campaign that harkened back to the days when organization and work were how political campaigns were waged.

In the past, when political parties were more than merely a branding label, the party provided a permanent organization. Structured parallel to government institutions and often more powerful and effective, the party was organized by states and broken down by counties, then wards, and finally precincts. Precinct captains knew their voters' names, families, and employers. More often than not the precinct captain was the one who made the jobs available, particularly government jobs, when their party was in power. At election time, precinct captains provided the manpower to canvass neighborhoods for party candidates, woo supporters, and make sure voters turned out on Election Day.

Today, the standing party organization does not reach so deeply into American society. Now candidates use money to achieve what used to be accomplished by the party organization. Consequently, most elections are won or lost by the fundraisers. They vote first, with their checkbooks, giving candidates the money to run phone banks, media advertisements, and e-mail blasts. Candidates who can't raise sufficient campaign funds find it impossible to compete and historically drop out when the money evaporates. When Sarah talks about "crony capitalism" and its effect on elections in America, this is what she means. Money drives most political campaigns. With it, the candidate wins. Without it, the candidate loses. Her campaigns ran contrary to that trend.

Even in 2006, when Sarah won the governor's race, most political consultants thought it was impossible to win an election without the backing of large political donors. That focus on an election system driven by money gives those large donors an inordinate amount of influence over politicians. Sarah campaigned for governor on a pledge to end that influence. To make good on her pledge, she had to find a way to campaign successfully without a lot of money. Her work ethic led her toward a different method, one that substituted the personal involvement of volunteers in place of political contributions. Doing that made it possible to keep her pledge to end big-donor influence and became a precursor to the future groundswell of grassroots campaigns that now has energized the conservative wing of the Republican Party. Thomas Jefferson once said, "I find that the harder I work the more luck I seem to have." The same could be said about Sarah.

Although she is not currently engaged in a political campaign, Sarah's day is plenty busy. Typically, her mornings begin with a five a.m. workout. Willow and Piper are still in school so on weekdays she helps them get ready and out the door. In the midst of that, she looks after Trig, catches up on current news, and reads the briefings of the day generated by advisers who work with her political action committee. She still does her own laundry and meal preparation and always has errands to run. Most days she spends several hours writing and, on days when she has a television appearance, she devotes much of her time to research for the show. Her e-mail in-box is always full, which requires considerable effort just to determine which messages to answer, forward, or delete. The early evening is spent with her family as everyone returns from their day and events operate in reverse—the children have dinner, homework, then off to bed. After that, the house gets quiet again and she spends time answering correspondence.

Work is the hallmark of Sarah's life. The accomplishments she's achieved and the success she's enjoyed didn't come from sitting idly by watching events unfold. She worked for it and she surrounded herself with family, friends, and supporters who were like-minded. That's not to say that she is a self-made politician. She couldn't have gone very far without the collaborative assistance of others, but she never asked anyone to do anything she wasn't willing to do or hadn't already done herself.

We shall endure because we live by that moral strength that we call grace. Because though we've often skirted a precipice, a Providential Hand has always guided us to a better future. So, let us seek that Hand once more.

Sarah Palin

CHAPTER 8

Faith

I find nothing in the language and ritual of the Church that speaks to me the way the mountains and the wilderness do.
CHUCK HEATH SR.

As with many aspects of our lives, faith and religion came to our family from several directions. Like streams flowing through the Alaskan wilderness, those influences followed a winding path before finding their way to us. I was not always conscious of how influential those spiritual roots might have been, but I was always aware that they were varied and diverse.

At times I struggled with meaning and purpose and why the events of my past turned out the way they did—my sister, Carol, and the years that passed without talking to her; and the almost nonexistent relationship with my father. I knew something about how those events happened and the facts that brought them to pass, but sometimes I wondered why and once in a while it troubled me. Now I think of that past as a rich heritage handed down to me by preceding generations, and one that I, however imperfectly, have passed on to our children.

Unlike my father, my mother, Nellie Marie Brandt Heath, who went by Marie, enjoyed a much less stressful childhood. Her father was heavily invested in the stock market and, until the Great Depression of 1929, enjoyed an affluent lifestyle from a large beachfront home in San Diego. They also had a home in Santa Monica. Unfortunately, most of that wealth evaporated in 1929, when the financial system crashed, but by then Marie was an adult and married to my father.

She attended the University of California–Berkeley, and earned a degree in English. After graduating, she began a teaching career at North Hollywood High School. She continued to teach after we moved to Idaho and enjoyed a career that spanned some forty-five years. Her former students remember her as easygoing, tolerant, and kind. That's how I remember her too. However, she was passionate and insistent about one thing—church.

As a devout member of the Church of Christ, Scientist, she attended worship services every Sunday and, while I was a young boy, she insisted that I accompany her. Founded by Mary Baker Eddy, the Church of Christ, Scientist, taught that sin, death, and disease were not created by God and therefore were an illusion. Only the spiritual life was real. Everything else—sickness, pain, disease—was nothing but a manifestation of evil and therefore deceptively nonexistent. According to the Church's teachings, by focusing on faith in God, believers could overcome the illusions of evil—sickness in particular—and find healing. Consequently, members of the Church routinely refused medical treatment.

My mother practiced that belief, at least to the extent of refusing medication, both for herself and for me. She did, on occasion, take me to the dentist, but I was not allowed to receive any drugs. That meant I had to endure the pain of dental work without the use of Novocain. I still cringe at the thought of going to the dentist, and especially at the sound of the drill.

As a young boy I often suffered from debilitating headaches.

Seeking medical care through a doctor was out of the question. My mother refused to give me even over-the-counter medication. Consequently, my only relief came from sleep. Then, around the time I turned fifteen, I discovered aspirin. That's when I abandoned even the pretense of agreement with Christian Science and forsook formal religion of any kind.

My father wanted little to do with it, either. He never objected to Mom attending Sunday services and even drove her into town so she could attend. But after he dropped her off at the church he went over to the café, where he spent the morning drinking coffee and telling stories. After I was old enough to refuse to attend, I spent Sundays hunting in the woods or fishing at the lake.

In Sally's family, things were a little less eclectic. Clem, her father, was a devout Catholic. He attended Mass daily throughout his adult life and insisted that all six of his children follow the ritual and teachings of the Church. They were baptized as infants, duly enrolled in catechism class, celebrated their first communion, and were confirmed by the bishop. Even when the family went on vacation they attended Mass at least once each week.

Clem also had a sense of humor and, although serious about his commitment to God, he held his religious beliefs with a light touch. Most mornings, he walked the two blocks up the street from their house to the church for morning Mass, then he caught a ride to the Spudnut Shop for a "spuddy" doughnut with his friends. One day his youngest son, Mike, commented about how faithful Clem was in attending church so regularly. With a twinkle in his eye, Clem replied, "How else could I get a ride to the doughnut shop?" It was a morning routine he followed six days a week—walk, Mass, Spuddy. He was a gentleman, always well dressed and well mannered, and he had a keen sense of humor that kept him smiling until the moment he died. Like everything else in his life, I'm sure that sense of humor came from the confidence he gained through a profound faith.

By contrast, the spiritual lineage of Sally's mother, Helen Sheeran, was shrouded in a little more mystery. She was born Helen Louise Gower in Wisconsin, in 1910. Around the time she turned fifteen, her mother abandoned the family and moved away. Helen and her brother, Homer, were sent to live with their grandparents. Later in life, after she was married and had children of her own, she received a phone call telling her that her mother resided in New York and was gravely ill. That was the first communication she'd received from her mother since the day she left the family. By the time Helen arrived in New York, her mother was dead.

When I knew her as my mother-in-law, Helen dutifully attended the Catholic Church. Her children—Sally and her siblings—said she was Episcopalian, yet members of Helen's extended family were Mormon. Although Helen made sure the children followed the rules and teachings of the Catholic Church and she accompanied them on Sundays to worship services, she held fast to her own beliefs until just a few months before she died. Near the end of her life she was stricken with cancer and gravely ill. One day the Catholic priest, while making his regular pastoral call, inquired about her faith and asked if she'd been baptized. "No," she replied. "But I would like to be." And so the priest baptized her at her home.

As Sarah rose through the political ranks from city council, to mayor, to governor, her strong religious commitment became known to news reporters and to the general public. Reporters looking for something to write about, and sometimes people I met on the street began to ask me about my faith. Even as a boy, when I attended church with my mother, I found little appealing in the organized religion to which I was exposed. My God was always the God of the mountains, the valleys, and the streams. I believed in God, as I do now. One could not scale the mountains or wade the rivers of Alaska and think it came from anywhere but God. I just don't care for organized religion. It's not that I think religious people are pretentious or hypocritical. People in every aspect of life are pretentious, and no one lives in a manner totally consistent with the things they claim to believe. I simply find nothing in the language and ritual of the Church that speaks to me about God the way the mountains and the wilderness do. When I pray, I pray to the One whose voice rumbles through the sky and roars down the mountainside.

Sitting on a pew for an hour doesn't reach me, but it has certainly been a means for God to work in Sally's life and in the lives of our children. When we first married, she faithfully attended Mass at the Catholic church every week. As my father did before me, I never opposed her participation and sometimes drove her to the services. When the children were born, she insisted that they be baptized in the Catholic Church. I attended those baptisms but rarely entered the building on other occasions.

After we moved to Alaska—first to Skagway and then on to Wasilla—Sally enrolled the children in catechism class. They attended faithfully, and if they ever expressed reluctance, I supported Sally's decision and made sure they knew that I expected them to do as they were told. As time went by, however, Sally's initial enthusiasm began to wane. I had no interest in attending church services, so going by herself meant wrangling three (and then very soon four) children on her own. By the time we made the move to Wasilla, their attendance had become less regular and they often went weeks and months without attending at all.

Even later, after the children were older and able to get themselves ready, logistics was still an issue. We only had one vehicle and I was usually gone on the weekends hunting, fishing, or guiding others through the mountains. On Sundays when they wanted to attend church, Sally and the children were forced to walk. Alaskan winters are bitterly cold and, as you might expect, the church they attended was chosen by how close it was to the house rather than by theological criteria. When we first moved to Wasilla, they attended the Presbyterian church, which was only about a quarter of a mile from our home.

Early in the 1970s, Sally got a job working as a secretary at the church. She took the job for the money, but she also was feeling spiritually unfulfilled. Most of her secretarial work was done at night, after we finished our evening routine at home. Alone in the church office, she had time to complete her tasks without interruption. She also had access to the pastor's library and began to read from his collection. At the same time, she inquired about other faiths. A friend of ours was a member of the Baha'i faith and they talked about what that meant, but what Sally learned of that religion failed to answer the longing of her spirit.

In January 1971, our friend Mary Ellan Moe invited Sally to attend a women's retreat. The event was held on a Saturday at Abbott Loop Chapel, a nondenominational congregation in Anchorage. When the day for the meeting arrived, Sally was at first reluctant to go and there were plenty of excuses available. It was bitterly cold and there were a thousand other things she could do with her Saturday, but Mary Ellan and her husband were good friends. Sally didn't want to let them down, so she got herself and the kids ready, then we headed out for the fifty-mile drive to Anchorage. Sally tells people I insisted she attend and goaded her into going. I don't remember doing that and if I did it, I don't remember why. I do remember that what happened to her that day changed our family forever.

At the time, most people who knew Sally thought she was already a Christian. I did. She had a kind and gentle disposition and was very nurturing. She also knew the language of the Church and could respond to other believers with the appropriate religious terms and phrases. For Sally, she was simply playing the part of a faithful believer. In her heart, however, she felt God was far from her.

As she sat through the conference that day in Anchorage, the Holy Spirit began to work in her mind and spirit, convincing her of her need for a personal relationship with God and challenging her to live a life of obedience to Him. By the end of the day she knew she needed to respond to what she'd heard and when the speaker offered an opportunity for prayer, Sally went forward. She was different after that. She seemed lighter on her feet and there was a new glow about her. And the change didn't melt away in the following weeks. If anything, the transformation grew deeper and she became more like the Sally we knew now than ever before.

At first, she didn't understand much about what had happened to her. Being "born again" was the new buzz phrase of the 1970s, but no one really understood what it meant. She tried to explain her experience to the Presbyterian pastor for whom she worked, but he seemed to understand only within a "church growth" framework. She wasn't aggressive in sharing her newfound faith with her old friends but when she did, some of them thought she was a little overboard. Finally, in an effort to figure out what had happened and what she needed to do next, she called Paul Riley, the pastor and founder of the Wasilla Assembly of God. She didn't know him at the time but she knew the church's reputation as a congregation that believed God was active in the world. Reverend

Riley knew exactly what had happened to her. "And no," he said, "you aren't crazy."

Shortly after that, Sally and the children began attending the Wasilla Assembly of God church. They were there three times a week—twice on Sunday and every Wednesday night. That summer they were all rebaptized in a service at Little Beaver Lake. I was there for the service.

Not long after that, the church hired Theron Horn as the youth director. Theron had a winsome personality and soon had quite a following. I liked him because he incorporated camping and hiking trips into the mountains as part of his program. He once told me about a trip the youth group took to the Russian River. Sarah was on that trip. It rained the entire time they were on the trail. Everyone was wet, tired, and hungry. Most of the kids groaned and complained, but there was Sarah, backpack on and cinched tight, ready for the day's hike. I don't doubt it for a minute. She took her first serious hiking trip when she was just seven years old. Hiked four days carrying a thirty-pound pack up the Chilkoot Trail. It was dubbed the "Golden Staircase" because it led to the headwaters of the Yukon River, a site where prospectors during the gold-rush days sought their fortune. That trail is thirty-five miles long and uphill most of the way from Dyea to Bennett Lake. Sarah climbed it all the way. That's what she was like. Always ready for what was next.

One Wednesday night during their regular youth program, Theron delivered a message to the group encouraging them to actually live what they believed. That night he said, "If you don't see yourself as a disciple and a follower of Christ, then this Christianity thing is worthless. Jesus called us to be involved in the world. Some of you are called to be professionals—doctors, lawyers, dentists—and some of you are called to work in government. We need Christians in government, and one of you may be the future president of the United States." Sarah was seated in the back of the room, watching and listening, and when Theron said the part about serving in government, he noticed her eyes light up. She didn't say anything and he never asked her about it, but he knew that what he'd said about Christians being involved in government struck a chord with her. That was perhaps the first time she considered the notion of politics as a calling for her life. Reporters have made fun of her sense of purpose, trying to suggest that she's some wild-eyed fanatic. In fact, she's just a woman who gets her sense of purpose from her relationship with God.

Many of the kids from school attended church with our children. Much has been written about the basketball team during Sarah's senior year. Most of those girls were Christians, but it wasn't because of Sarah. It was because of the leadership Theron Horn provided through the youth group at the church and the continual support Rodger Foreman, the high school wrestling coach, gave them on campus. With their help, the group of girls who were Christians included more than just Sarah's team. For a period of ten years that stretched from Heather's class, a year ahead of Sarah, all the way through the class of our youngest daughter, Molly, four classes later, the girls' teams did well and produced excellent records. Most of those girls were Christians.

Throughout her life, Sarah has been supported in her faith by friends and acquaintances who have taken it upon themselves to assist her with prayer and advice. As a young girl she had the guidance of her mother, Sally, and of her youth pastor, Theron Horn. She was greatly influenced by the ministry of Paul Riley and his wife, Helen. When she entered the race for mayor of Wasilla, a group of women at the church organized a prayer group to pray and intercede specifically for Sarah. That group included Melanie Messenger, a friend who came to Alaska from Oregon in 1984.

Throughout Sarah's term as mayor, Melanie and the prayer group met regularly, sometimes with Sarah present and sometimes without her even knowing they were gathering, and they continued to support her after she became governor. As that effort ran its course, another group emerged that still meets regularly to pray for her. No one asked them to. They did it on their own as a way of being involved from a spiritual side. I don't know what they talk about at those meetings—they wouldn't tell me if I asked—but I know that their support gives Sarah an assurance that she is not alone in the work she does or in the challenges she faces.

And I am so proud to be the daughter of Chuck and Sally Heath.

Sarah Palin

CHAPTER 9

Family

*Now, when you hear Sarah's one-liners . . . you know
where she got them.*
CHUCK HEATH JR.

We grew up in a household marked by an interest in sports and the outdoors. Hunting, fishing, track and field, basketball, football, wildlife, and camping got most of our attention. Yet in spite of the common interests we shared, we each had our own distinct personality.

Heather was sensitive, quiet, and the hardest worker of us all. A perfectionist, she could never settle for anything less than an A on an assignment. She also was very much the older sister and the one most often found in the kitchen baking with Mom. While attending Northwest Nazarene College, she was nominated for a Rhodes scholarship but declined to apply. She just wanted to get her degree in speech pathology, come back to Alaska, and help children.

Molly, our youngest sister, was the most naturally gregarious and could find humor in almost any situation. I tried to be funny, but expectations were a little different for me. I was the eldest child and the only boy. Most of the things I remember weren't about me being funny but about being awkward. I was curious, rambunctious, and broke almost every bone in my body.

Living in a small house, we grew up in close proximity to one another. That led to hotly contested disputes between us, but also made us very protective. Once, while waiting for the school bus to arrive, a boy named Chris Troseth started picking on Sarah. Chris was bigger and stronger, but I jumped in his face and told him I was going to beat him up if he didn't leave her alone. Surprisingly, he backed down. I remember later wondering why I risked my own safety to stick up for Sarah when she drove me crazy most of the time. Even today, it's difficult to stand quietly by when I hear the ridiculous lies that are constantly spread about her.

When I'm out in public, and people find out I'm from Alaska, they usually ask what I think of Sarah Palin. I normally tell them she was a terrific governor and did great things for our state. Often, people who bring up the subject are only looking for an opportunity to make the usual erroneous allegations—she banned books from the public library, believes that dinosaurs and men coexisted just a few thousand years ago, and that she is not really Trig's mother. Countering those allegations requires a careful review of the facts, and most of the time I give them that careful review. Confronted with the truth, they shake their heads in disbelief and say, "There is no way the national news media would make up all those things." That's the most infuriating part of it. Not that people believe what the news media says, but that the news media gets away with so many mistakes and outright false statements. I still feel the same tension I felt when Chris Troseth was picking on her at the bus stop, but I have learned I can't beat sense into everyone.

When Sarah was born she was round and pink with a shock of black hair. Dad commented that she looked like a bulldog. Paul Drinkwater, a reporter for the *Sandpoint News-Bulletin*, quoted him as saying he was going to name her Oscar and raise her like a tomboy. He didn't name her Oscar but he did raise her like a tomboy.

The strength of Sarah's character became evident at a very early age. After she entered politics, a reporter asked Dad about his influence over Sarah's views and opinions. He said, "My ability to influence her ended when she was two years old." That was an exaggeration, but only slightly. Stubbornness runs in the Heath family. Once we've made up our mind, nothing much will change it. Sarah was the most stubborn of us all.

When we were children, Dad's word was the law in our household and everyone was expected to do as he said. He was an imposing figure and we wouldn't dare argue with him or question his authority...except Sarah. She never really disobeyed him, but she didn't hesitate to stand up for herself either. Many times I cringed as they stood toe-to-toe in a heated debate about what she was or was not going to do. She rarely backed down and most of the time, she was right. I was amazed that she got away with it. Grandma Heath used to say, "There's something really different about Sarah. Someday, she is going to do something very special." That statement stayed with me over the years and I often wondered what she would become. She had a fearlessness the rest of us didn't have.

Sarah didn't mind getting her hands dirty either. She always jumped right in when we cleaned animals and packed meat. She was not a "girly" girl at all, which I found quite ironic when she later entered the Miss Wasilla beauty pageant. When she was in college and dating Todd, she joined him on the boat during the commercial fishing season and worked the net like a seasoned hand. I've seen her bone tired from it but I've never heard her complain.

She also had a sharp eye for details. When we were children,

Dad used to take us for a ride around Wasilla. Not many people lived there then and wild animals often roamed through the neighborhood. For something to do, we often piled into the car and cruised around looking for them. It was a cheap form of entertainment and an easy way to fill the freezer. Dad used to tell us, "I'll give you five dollars if you see a bull moose and I can shoot it." On one of those rides, we were about five miles outside Wasilla when a cow moose sauntered across the road. We all shouted and pointed, but Dad kept driving. Sarah piped up, "Aren't you going to shoot it?" Dad explained to her that it was a cow. "No, it's not," Sarah argued. "It's a bull." Dad handed her the binoculars and pointed in the direction he'd been looking. "See for yourself," he said, his patience wearing a little thin.

"Not that one," Sarah replied. Then she pointed to the left. "I mean that one." Sure enough, a bull moose was standing about fifty or sixty yards off the road. Dad took the rifle, stepped away from the car, and dropped it with a single shot. And Sarah pocketed five dollars.

One thing that didn't emerge until much later in life was her sense of humor. As kids we laughed a lot, sometimes to the point of tears, when we watched television or a movie, but the use of humor as a means of communicating came later for Sarah. As a politician she became known as a champion of the Reagan one-liner. She used several in her acceptance speech at the 2008 Republican National Convention and a few of them got her into trouble with liberals and the media. That kind of sharp, pithy, often humorous quip became an effective tool for Sarah on the campaign trail. However, from childhood through high school she was noted for discipline, tenacity, and hard work. She was a serious person and not at all interested in a glib, lighthearted view of life.

When she was in elementary school, Dad would bring in the newspaper and take out the sports section. While everyone else asked about the results of the latest game, Sarah was busy reading the front-page articles about world events. In Alaska, especially during the 1960s and 1970s, keeping up with current events wasn't an easy task. Most major events on television were broadcast on a tape delay, which meant we didn't see them until two or three days after the event had occurred. Even watching real-time newscasts took special effort. The five o'clock news from New York, broadcast simultaneously to us, reached Alaska television sets at one o'clock in the afternoon, while we were in class. By the time Sarah got home from school, it was already eight o'clock in the evening on the East Coast.

Still, events of the world mattered to her and seemed always on her mind, cropping up in comments and conversation, sometimes at the oddest moments. Our friend Marie Carter remembered working with Sarah in the summer of 1981. They were clearing trails and cleaning picnic areas at Nancy Lake. One afternoon in July they were sitting out a rainstorm in a canvas tent. As they watched the rain through the flap, Sarah quipped, "We're out here, working in the rain, and Princess Diana is getting married today." Marie hadn't noticed the date, but Sarah had noticed it and remembered.

Humor might not have defined Sarah, but it is a large part of the Alaskan persona and an important part of our parents' personalities. Not the kind that results in a joke but as an orientation toward life. It provides a way of making the challenges of weather, terrain, and finances less intimidating. For Alaskans, laughing at danger and death puts things in a more manageable perspective and frees our minds to find creative solutions to the problems those circumstances pose. We laugh about a lot of things and set even the mundane events of life in a humorous context, whether it fits or not.

Once when Sarah was in high school, the girls' track team had an early-morning trip for a meet in Kenai. Our family enjoys hot coffee, so while Dad was gathering his things for the trip, he went to the garage and took a thermos from the shelf. He brought it into the house and, without rinsing it or looking inside, filled it with hot coffee. The bus ride that morning took three or four hours and along the way, Mom, Dad, and Sarah kept themselves warm by sipping coffee from the thermos. As it turned out, Mom got the last cupful. When Sarah tilted the thermos to drain the last drops into Mom's cup, a dead mouse plopped out. They shrieked and howled, then doubled over in laughter at the realization they'd drunk the coffee all morning with the mouse floating around in it.

Frank Gurtler is an Alaskan native who grew up on the banks of the Yukon River in the village of Ruby. A popular musician, he also is a well-known hunting and fishing guide who continues to work today, even though he's in his seventies. One night, Frank came to visit us at a cabin on the Tanana River. We were sitting around the campfire telling stories when suddenly, Frank, who had been leaning back in his chair, fell over backward and tumbled twenty feet down an embankment to the river. All but his right hand was submerged beneath the water and in it was the can of beer he'd been drinking, held high to keep it dry. Seconds later, Frank's head popped to the surface. He gestured with the can and grinned. "Didn't spill a drop!"

That's the kind of humor Alaskans cherish. Our parents enjoyed it and did their best to convey it to us. They rarely let an opportunity for a good laugh pass, even if it came at our expense. During the winter when I was in first grade, I came home from school tired and exhausted. I dropped my book bag near the door, tottered off to the bedroom, and took a nap. When I awoke, it was dark outside. In the winter, it gets dark in most parts of southern Alaska by four in the afternoon and the sun doesn't come up until after ten in the morning. Refreshed from the nap, I rolled off the bed, got dressed, and went to the kitchen, where I asked for a bowl of oatmeal. Mom prepared it for me and while I ate she packed my regular lunch. By then, Dad was in the kitchen watching. After eating the bowl of oatmeal, I grabbed my book bag, hugged them both good-bye, and headed across the street to the Lawsons' house like I did every morning to walk to school with their children. When I knocked on the front door Mrs. Lawson opened it with a puzzled look and asked me what I wanted. I said I was there to pick up the boys for the walk to school. She laughed and said it was nine o'clock at night. I was embarrassed and angry with my parents for playing that trick on me, but that's the kind of humor they enjoyed. Their friends were often the object of that humor too.

Dad competed in more than a dozen marathons, including the 1982 Boston Marathon. He trained hard for the event and when it was over he had plenty of stories to tell and didn't mind sharing them, whether people wanted to listen or not. One of his friends, a fellow runner named Ron Moore, enjoyed running as much as Dad and he was always talking about his finishing time in the latest event. Dad thought Ron was bragging too much, so in an effort to make his point, Dad entered a local 10K run under Ron's name. Then he purposely ran slower than everyone else and came in dead last. The results were published in the newspaper for all to see. Not to be outdone, Ron found a way to get even.

Our father is a collector of just about everything. If you go to his house, the first thing you'll notice is a stack of antlers standing by the driveway. It's more than eight feet tall and made primarily from antlers that he and others found in the woods. Some came from moose and caribou he killed but many were antlers the animals shed naturally. Across the yard from the antler stack is a dog pen made with a chain-link fence. The fence is covered with orange and white floats he picked up while walking the beach. Inside the garage, shelves line the wall all the way to the ceiling. The shelves are filled with one-gallon jars packed full of fishing lures we pulled from stumps and logs in the creeks and rivers where we fished in the summer. Dad organized them by size and shape and stored them in the jars.

After the newspaper published the results of the race showing Ron Moore's name in last place, Ron placed an advertisement in the classified section of the paper. The ad announced that Chuck Heath was disposing of his lure collection and anyone who lost a lure recently could come by the house and pick it up. When people showed up at the garage looking for their lures, Dad knew something was up. It didn't take long to figure out who was behind it.

One April Fool's Day when he was teaching at Iditarod Elementary School in Wasilla, Dad prepared letters to all his fellow teachers. Sent out under the name of the principal, the letters reprimanded each teacher for something they supposedly did and demanded that they appear at the office after school to address the matter. When classes finished for the day, the teachers lined up outside the principal's office and wanted to know why they were being wrongfully accused. They were irate until someone figured out Dad was the only teacher missing and realized they'd been had.

Dad became known for his practical jokes, which often served to make life interesting for his fellow teachers. As Ray Carter, the principal, said, "You didn't want to miss a day at school." My favorite joke, however, was the time he ran an advertisement in the newspaper for a prayer line using Ron Moore's telephone number. Now, when you hear Sarah's one-liners like "The difference between a hockey mom and a pit bull: lipstick," or, "I'm not quitting, I'm just reloading," you know where she got them.

We learned to appreciate Dad's sense of humor, but one thing we never got used to was his choice of automobiles. When we first moved to Wasilla he had an AMC Rebel. While driving through McKinley Park we hit a rock and knocked a hole in the gas tank. The hole was big enough to stick your fist in and the gasoline quickly drained out. A park ranger helped us rig a five-gallon gas can in the trunk and we limped home. When we arrived back in town, Dad went to a junkyard to find a new tank. They didn't have one for that model so he took one that was small enough to fit inside the trunk, secured it in place, and connected the gas line. It worked great except that when we stopped at the gas station to fill up we had to lift the trunk lid to reach the filler cap. That doesn't sound like much now, but back then it was embarrassing. We did our best to avoid being in the car when we knew he was stopping for gas.

A few years later, he had a blue 1972 Ford station wagon. It was long and clunky and had a few dents, but the biggest problem was the spare tire he kept strapped to the top. When he drove us to school in the mornings we had him stop a few blocks away so we could get out and walk. We didn't want our friends to see us in the car.

The worst car he owned was a Datsun 310. It was dented and banged up so much the driver's door wouldn't open. To get inside we had to crawl through from the passenger side. Dad used it on hunting trips and to haul things. None of us would ride in it. When the car reached what we thought were its final days, Dad parked it in the woods near our house. It sat there for three years until one summer Sarah made friends with a couple of Mormon missionaries. When they completed their mission, they needed a way to get back home and asked if they could buy the old Datsun. Dad gave it to them instead. All four tires were flat and the battery was dead but we got it running and they headed south. Four days later they called to tell us they'd reached Utah without any trouble.

As Sarah got older, her serious and disciplined perspective mellowed some, especially after she and Todd began to have a family. Rearing children of her own brought out the nurturing side of her personality. Still, when she had something to say, she had a way of getting right to the point.

In the 1990s, while exploring the bush for fossils with Dad, I came across some flecks of gold in a creek bed. We had friends who were full-time gold miners and I had heard stories from the gold-rush days about the fortunes made and lost in the Alaska wilderness. Hearing about gold is one thing, seeing it in your hand is another. Once I held it in my hand, I was hooked. If gold was that easy to find, I reasoned, then why was I wasting my time doing anything else?

Over the next several years I returned to mine along creeks and rivers I thought were promising locations. Each time, I brought more elaborate equipment with me. First a pan, then a shovel and sluice box. Finally, in 1997, I convinced myself I could make a living mining full-time. I moved to the bush, set up camp, and went after my fortune. By then I'd moved on from the shovel and sluice box to a gasoline-powered dredge.

In the warm months I wore shorts and a T-shirt and waded in the mud all day. During winter, I donned a dry suit and worked the dredge beneath the ice, sucking ore-laden gravel from the bedrock. My fingers bled from scraping against the river bottom and my lips swelled to twice their normal size from exposure. Most days, summer or winter, I came from the water chilled to the bone and shivered for hours as I tried to get warm. But at night, I sat alone and stared up at the stars and thought I was in heaven. I was miles from the nearest town and never wanted to return to life in the city.

One day, in the midst of that wild adventure, Sarah came out to see me. She listened attentively as I gushed on and on about life in the wilderness and the thrill of mining for gold. I was doing it—I was mining and making at least as much money as I made teaching school. That afternoon, standing on the banks of the river as the sun sank low in the sky toward the crest of the mountain, she turned to me and said, "You need to get back to town. You're becoming a hermit."

I didn't want to hear those words, but one glance in a mirror told me she was right. My hair was long and stringy. My beard was rough and scraggly and I looked like some of the men I'd seen on the trail, their eyes filled with that faraway gaze, as if their mind was a million miles away even when they were staring straight at you. Not long after her visit, I packed up and started for home.

That's the way we are as a family. We don't hang out with one another that much and we aren't always minding one another's business. If you come to Alaska expecting to find the Heath family anything like the Waltons of television fame, you'll be sorely disappointed. But we're watching from the corner of our eye and we know who's in trouble and which one of us needs a hand.

No, the road isn't easy, but it's
nothing compared to the suffering
and sacrifice of those who
came before us.

Sarah Palin

CHAPTER 10

Running

Each Saturday we gathered with other families in the
Mat-Su Valley for a leisurely five-mile run.
CHUCK HEATH SR.

After Sally and I married, teaching became my full-time job and a lifetime profession, but sports was still a big part of my life. In Idaho, I'd coached junior high football, basketball, and track. Following our move to Skagway, I taught grades five, six, and seven during the academic year, drove a taxi, and tended bar. During my free time I hunted for mountain goats and seals. I also discovered town basketball.

Basketball was big in Alaska, and many towns in the southeastern part of the state had adult basketball teams that traveled. In spite of Skagway's inaccessibility (at the time we lived there it was accessible only by air or water), the town team traveled around the region to play teams from Whitehorse, Juneau, Haines, and other locations. All the team members had full-time jobs and participation was unpaid and voluntary. We had to cover the costs ourselves, including the cost of travel. Traveling also meant I was occasionally absent from the classroom, but because we represented the town, the school district approved those absences and continued to pay me for the days I was gone. I spent four years playing on the team. One of the highlights for me was playing in the Yukon Sourdough Rendezvous basketball tournament.

In 1972, the Summer Olympic Games were held in Munich, Germany. Coverage of the games was broadcast on television in the United States by the ABC network. Like many families in the nation, we watched as Frank Shorter won the marathon. No American had won that event since 1908. Many still remember the conclusion of the race when an imposter ran into the stadium ahead of Shorter in an attempt to steal his moment of victory. The intruder was eventually herded out of the way and Shorter crossed the finish line to win.

By some estimates, Shorter's success in those games inspired as many as twenty-five million people to take up the sport of distance running. Regardless of the exact numbers or whether his win had much to do with it, the 1970s saw a dramatic increase in the popularity of running, both as a sport and as personal recreation. That running craze reached all the way to our tiny village of Wasilla when George Brown organized Family Fun Runs. Each Saturday we gathered with other families in the Mat-Su Valley for a leisurely five-mile run along the highways near our home.

When we first moved to Wasilla, I was still teaching at the school in Chugiak. Later, I moved to Iditarod Elementary not far from our house. That move allowed me to coach at Wasilla High School. I was head coach for the girls' track and cross-country teams. Don Teeguarden, head coach for the girls' basketball team, assisted me. To help the girls with training, we ran alongside them in practice. I had been a sprinter in high school and thought that distance runners were crazy. Being forced to run with them as a coach changed my mind and I actually enjoyed the experience.

Running also helped me get ready for hunting trips. I worked as a guide back then and being in better shape than my client was always an advantage. The weather in Alaska can change almost instantly and when trouble comes, the guide is the one who has to come up with a solution. Being in top shape can sometimes mean the difference between living and dying.

When I ran at times other than track team or cross-country practice, I took the children with me. I could usually push them past their comfort level and when they started hurting I told them all those things coaches tell their players like, "No pain, no gain," and "It's just the weakness leaving your body." It sounds kind of corny today, and a little like the Christian Scientist dogma I heard from my mother when I was growing up, but at least it gave them a different perspective on their experience. It *was* the weakness leaving their bodies, at least in one sense—if they pushed themselves past the pain, their endurance would increase and they would grow stronger.

I also told them things like, "Everybody hurts in a race. Winners are the ones who can block out that hurt and focus on the end result." That statement is absolutely true, and not just for athletes. Every person—sportsman, artist, dancer, whatever the endeavor—encounters pain in one form or another. The best ones learn to thrive on it by pushing past it. Learning to ignore adversity is an essential key to success. It sounds a little Kafkaesque—like "A Hunger Artist" pushing himself to the brink of death just to prove how good he is—but avoiding pain, as a primary goal, is a recipe for failure.

One day while we were training with the cross-country team, Teeguarden suggested we should run a marathon. I was intrigued by the idea but at 26 miles, 385 yards, the distance was intimidating. Rather than yield to that intimidation, I pushed back and agreed to run with him. We began running regularly, gradually extending the length until we could run the required distance. A few months later we entered a marathon in Anchorage. I was amazed we actually completed the distance. We continued to train and later in the year we ran another race. By then I was an avid participant in the sport of distance running and began to think about running in a nationally recognized event. My attention turned to the Boston Marathon.

Held each year on the third Monday in April, the Boston Marathon began in 1897. Like the running craze of the 1970s, the enthusiasm that swept the nation in the 1800s followed the return of the marathon as an event in the 1896 Olympic Games. To qualify for the Boston Marathon, runners must participate in a marathon sanctioned by an organization affiliated with the International Association of Athletics Federation, an international body that governs amateur sports. At that event, the runner must complete the race with a finishing time that meets a minimum time set by the Boston Athletics Club. Those minimum times are adjusted according to age groups. In 1982, I was forty-four years old. In order to qualify I had to complete a sanctioned marathon in less than three hours, ten minutes.

That year I decided to make a qualifying run in the Glacier Marathon, a race held on the Turnagain Arm, a branch of Cook Inlet, south of Anchorage, not far from the place where our friend was killed in that avalanche I told you about earlier. The race was held early in the day in order to avoid the high winds that often pick up later in the afternoon. I began that race at seven in the morning. My time was three hours, six minutes, just fast enough to qualify for the Boston Marathon. That was a finish time I would never repeat.

I filed an application with the Boston Athletics Club and waited. A few weeks later I received a letter from them notifying me that my application had been received and I was included in the field for that year's race. There was only one problem. As with many other times in my life, I was long on dreams and short on money. There was no way I could pay for a trip like that.

Sally and I had been coaching the girls' track team at Wasilla High School for a number of years. We didn't have much in the way of track-and-field facilities but did our best to get the girls ready for events. Most of our training was conducted on the highway or through the woods. I pushed the girls at practice, always trying to get them to do better, and then I shouted and yelled like a madman at track meets. Some coaches do just the opposite. I was more like Cotton Barlow of my high school days. I wasn't mean, I just wanted them to do better and to know that I had their best interests at heart. Little did I know, the feeling was mutual.

When the girls on the team learned that I had been accepted for the Boston Marathon, they were overjoyed. Rather than simply congratulate me, though, they did something tangible to show their appreciation. They organized a fund-raising effort and purchased airline tickets for Sally and me to make the trip to Boston.

With the track team cheering me on from back in Wasilla, we traveled east for the event. I finished an hour behind the winner, Alberto Salazar, who completed the course in two hours, eight minutes, fifty-two seconds, which was a course record. I was just glad and thankful to have completed the race.

That was the crowning achievement of my running career, but it wasn't my last race. I continued to run that year and throughout the remainder of the 1980s. In 1985, I ran in the Stroh's Run for Liberty to celebrate the Statue of Liberty and its approaching centennial commemoration. A few years later, I was on a relay team for the 1987 and 1988 Klondike Trail of '98 International Road Relay, a 110-mile race from Skagway to Whitehorse. Heather ran that race as part of a women's team in 1990, and repeated it in 1992, on a mixed team with her husband.

During that same period, the Russian national cross-country team arrived in Wasilla for the Hatcher Pass Relay, a 50K race up Hatcher Pass. Normally a ten-man team, one of their members could not make the trip. We housed several of the team members at our home and when they learned I was a runner, they asked me to join them to fill in for their missing teammate. I ran one leg of the race and helped them finish in a respectable time, but I was the slowest member of the team.

Running in the Boston Marathon was one of my biggest ideas, but I wasn't the only one in the family for whom running spawned grandiose dreams. Early in the 1990s, while on a trip to France, Chuck Jr. saw a portion of the Tour de France bicycle race. As he watched the cyclists speeding by, jockeying for position and then pumping their way up and over the hills of the French country-side, he became engrossed in the idea of one day competing in the race. It wasn't a running sport but it drew on the same athletic qualities—endurance and determination. He'd been fast most of his life as a sprinter and as he watched the race that day he became convinced he could translate his experience as a runner and football player into the skills necessary to compete as a cyclist.

Over the next few days, the idea of doing it became a commitment and when he returned home from the trip, he started training to be a bicycle racer. He competed in a number of races sponsored by the Arctic Bicycle Club and slowly worked his way up to a second-place ranking in the men's expert class.

For several years he continued racing and training, trying to transform his body from football player to professional cyclist and hoping for a spot on a cycling team, but living in Alaska limited his ability to train year-round. He was also limited by his body type. Beginning as a teenager, he had spent hours in the weight room training to gain the muscle necessary to play football, a sport that values size and strength. Bicycle racing emphasizes endurance and values a sleek, slender physique. Although he was in good physical shape, his size added extra weight, which slowed his times significantly.

Still, he continued training hard until two serious crashes put him in the hospital. The first, a cycling accident, happened when the front wheel came off his bicycle and the fork dug into the pavement, sending him sailing over the handlebars. He knew he was in trouble when, during the ride to the hospital, the EMT in the ambulance said, "There are amazing things that doctors can do with plastic surgery nowadays." In the emergency room, they used tweezers to pull pavement from his scalp.

That accident left him gun-shy of racing and he found it difficult to give the kind of effort winning required. A subsequent car wreck injured muscles in his neck and left him unable to hold his head in a cycling position for the extended periods of time required to race. Nowadays, he confines his athletic effort to playing hockey on a team that competes with men his own age. It's not much safer than cycling but it's a sport he knows and understands.

Running also had an effect on Sally. She grew up in an athletic family but as a young girl she turned toward other interests. Back then, high schools had cheerleaders and song leaders. Sally was a song leader and led the audience at sports events in singing fight songs. Later she tried golf, but it wasn't a big part of her life. When she met me I tried to interest her in sports but she was mostly interested in watching. After running in some of the Family Fun Runs on Saturdays, she got interested in the sport of distance competition.

The first time she went out for a run she made it about three blocks without stopping. She came back to the house happy and proud to have made it that far. The next day, she made it a little farther and by the end of the week she ran a mile without stopping. She and her friends Linda, Toni, and Valerie began running together, no matter the weather, with the goal of competing in a marathon. A year later, Sally ran in her first and only marathon, the Anchorage Mayor's Marathon. She was inspired that day by Marcie Trent, the seventy-year-old veteran runner who competed with her in that race. Sally finished the course in four hours, thirty minutes. Not bad. I know plenty of people who couldn't do it in twice that time.

Although she never ran another marathon, she ran in a number of long-distance races. While watching one of Sally's races in Anchorage, Heather met the man who would become her husband.

Some writers have suggested I pushed our girls to run track and cross-country, and that I badgered them as their coach. The part about badgering them is not true, though I did push them to do more. Coaches often say, "There's nothing more difficult than coaching your own child—except playing for your parent." That was true of us. Don Teeguarden remembered Heather complaining, "I don't like it when coaches stand by the track and yell, 'Run faster.'" She was talking about me. As I mentioned earlier, I tended to get rather emotionally involved in the meets and I'm sure it was particularly difficult for my children to accept. Someone else can jump and shout and yell at a sports event, but when it's your parent, it's different. I understand that, but I never badgered them any more than I did anyone else. The part about pointing them toward running was a different matter.

When I began coaching the girls' track and cross-country teams, Heather and Sarah were playing volleyball as a fall sport.

I pushed them toward distance running because I was coach of the girls' team and the team needed their help. The two sports, volleyball and cross-country, shared the same season. They couldn't participate in both. My insistence that they join the track and cross-country teams kept them off the volleyball team. If that was wrong, then I was wrong. But the experience was not a loss. They gained lifelong fitness skills that have served them well in adulthood and they learned to apply themselves to a difficult task, overcome the odds, and achieve a goal.

Every athlete has to learn to work the hardest on the things they perform poorly at, without losing proficiency at the things they do well. That's how they improve. For Sarah, one of the events she worked at the hardest was the hurdles. Getting her arms, legs, and torso in the proper position took hours and hours of practice. She didn't start out so well, but by her senior year she was doing great. Even now, when I look at pictures of Heather and Sarah running the hurdles, I have a deep sense of pride and satisfaction. Their form was perfect.

I still enjoy running, especially in extreme conditions. Chuck Jr. and I went for a run once in Fairbanks when the temperature was forty-two degrees below zero. The condensation from our breath froze instantly and covered our faces with frost. By the time we finished, we had icicles hanging from our nostrils, eyelashes, and eyebrows. We looked like wild men. People who know us might say that's not far from the truth.

Running on a windy day can be fun, too, which is a good thing because the wind often blows hard in the Matanuska Valley. I never let it stop me. Instead, I make it work in my favor. Running against the wind increases the resistance and makes me stronger. That's also an apt metaphor for the way Sarah has run her political life—against the wind. It's been a challenge for her. I can only hope it's made her stronger. Sarah and Heather still run for the fun of it too.

Recently, Sarah participated in a half-marathon at Storm Lake, Iowa. She registered under her maiden name, Sarah Heath, and started near the back of the crowd. With a running visor and sunglasses, no one noticed her until the race was about to start. She finished the event in one hour, forty-six minutes and came in second in her age group. At the time, political pundits were speculating about whether she would run for president. Participants in the Storm Lake race were wondering if she was considering a run in the Boston Marathon. I don't know any more about her political ambitions than anyone else, so I can't help with the political prognostication. I *do* know something about marathons, though, and to qualify for the Boston Marathon she'll need to trim a little off that time. I am confident she can do it. She was always diligent at training and preparation.

I will remember all the young girls who came up to me at our rallies, sometimes taking off from school, just to see only the second woman ever nominated by a major party in a national election. They know that in America there should be no ceilings on achievement, glass or otherwise.

Sarah Palin

CHAPTER 11

Chart Your Own Course

*Many of his former pupils still talk about what they learned
through the hands-on experience in his class.*
CHUCK HEATH JR.

In 1972, Dad was teaching sixth grade at the school in Chugiak. A new principal, Mari Rich, was scheduled to arrive that year and Dad went to school early to meet her. Instead of introducing himself, he posed as an irate parent who was upset at the way his children were treated. He made numerous accusations about the school in general and then he said, "What about this Heath guy? I hear he's a real jerk." Mari didn't know Dad, but she stood up for him and defended him—and won Dad's undying allegiance. Her support proved critical not just with parents but with the school board. Dad had an idea for a new curriculum he wanted to write and then use with his sixth-grade class, one that required school-board approval. Mari's support was crucial in that effort.

In most school systems today, students are evaluated by standardized, state-issued tests. How well students perform on those tests determines not only whether they pass or fail, but goes a long way in determining their academic future. It also affects the school's future too. Often, state and federal funding depend on where students rank in their performance on those tests. In the process, teaching as a means of inspiring students to learn is lost in the drive to prepare students for the next examination. Teachers teach for the questions that will appear on the test, rather than for the love of the subject matter. Dad would have none of that.

In an effort to inspire his students, he designed a curriculum for the sixth grade that integrated every subject into preparation for a year-end extended camping trip at Mount McKinley, a trip that included the entire sixth grade, not just his class. With Mari's help, he wrote detailed lesson plans for each subject, created special projects that trained students in the skills they needed for the trip, and devised safeguards to ensure no one was injured. After reviewing the curriculum and fine-tuning a few points, Mari presented it to the school board. With her support, it won approval.

That year, and for several years that followed, sixth-grade math moved from an exercise in numbers to real-life calculations—the distance from Wasilla to Mount McKinley, how long the trip would take at various speeds, and the amount of gasoline needed to complete the journey. Dad took backpacks to school and loaded them with weight, then taught his students to measure the amount of work necessary to carry that pack up the mountain. They estimated the amount of food necessary to sustain the group, determined the cost of the trip, and kept track of fund-raising efforts to meet those costs.

The same thing happened with other subjects as well. History became a yearlong exploration of the state of Alaska and the significance of Mount McKinley, a mountain named for a US president who never visited the state. Reading concentrated on the lives of Alaskan explorers and especially those who explored the area around the mountain. In science class, students learned about the plants and animals they would see on the trip and the kind of weather they might expect to experience there.

As part of their preparation, students were required to complete a survival course that taught them how to live in the Alaskan outdoors. They learned how to endure rain, snow, and subzero weather. Then they got to experience it on an overnight winter camping trip. Typically that trip came on one of the coldest nights of the year. The kids had to build their own snow caves to sleep in and start their own fires to cook over. Heather, Sarah, Molly, and I were expected to accompany Dad on the year-end trip, so we had to pass the survival course too.

Enthusiasm for the trip spilled over from the classroom into the homes of Dad's students. By the end of the year, every parent wanted to accompany the class. Many of them did just that, along with carefully chosen chaperones who could contribute special expertise to the trip.

People still talk about those trips, but that wasn't the only interesting thing Dad did in the classroom. From the time we moved to Alaska, we hunted, fished, and trapped year-round. Most of what we killed or caught went straight to the freezer. Pelts from animals taken off the trapline, and many from animals we killed while hunting, were sold for cash. It was business as much as pleasure. Animals killed on the trail were butchered, either right where they lay or back at our camp. Once we got home, the meat was cut into useable portions and wrapped for storage. The major organs, however, went with Dad to his classroom where they were dissected and studied by his class.

On winter weekends we hunted ptarmigan. Dad often took the gizzards and feet to class the following Monday. The birds had no teeth, so they swallowed small pebbles that accumulated as grist in their gizzard. They used it to grind up their food. Ptarmigan are attracted to shiny objects. Occasionally hunters find gold nuggets in the birds' gizzards. Dad's students never found any gold, but we did find a penny once, which had been worn almost beyond recognition.

In the fall we killed moose to provide meat for the winter. That gave Dad's students an even more dramatic lesson. He spread out plastic sheets on the classroom tables and set up stations with the heart, liver, kidneys, lungs, and eyeballs. The kids learned to identify the different parts and their functions. It was a little gross when they hooked a hand pump to the lungs to watch them inflate, but the visual effect made a deep impression on the students. Many of his former pupils still talk about what they learned through the hands-on experience in his class.

One winter we caught a coyote on our trapline. After we skinned it for the pelt, Dad took the carcass to class. Under his watchful eye, the students dissected the animal, learning where each organ lay in the cavity and how they were connected together. His classroom was located on the second floor of the school building and when the students weren't using the carcass, he hung it outside the window to keep it cold. A student from another classroom asked Dad what kind of animal it was and Dad replied in jest, "It's Rufus, our German Shepherd."

The kid went home and told his parents, who promptly called an animal-rights organization. A few days later, representatives from the group came to school to investigate. They dropped the case when they heard the real story. However, that wasn't the only time he got into trouble for his use of animals in the classroom.

As part of his science curriculum Dad taught a unit on rocketry. Students learned how rockets were made and studied things like trajectory, speed, and flight duration. During the 1970s the space program still captured the imagination of many Americans. Dad's rocketry class was popular with the students. The curriculum culminated with "Launch Day," when the students spent their class time launching rockets from the playground. One year, Dad allowed some of his students to insert live gerbils into the clear plastic payload sections of their rockets and launch them hundreds of feet into the air. The gerbils safely parachuted back to earth and the kids thought it was great until one of the parachutes failed and the gerbil plunged to a crash landing. After parents learned what happened, the space-gerbil program was canceled.

One year the class project included a reenactment of the Pilgrims' first Thanksgiving feast. The girls baked pies, cooked vegetables, and decorated the classroom. A live turkey was donated to the class by a local farmer, and the boys were in charge of its care. On the appointed day for the feast, they took the turkey to the playground and beheaded it. Then they plucked it clean, dressed it, and cooked it. Travis Bradley, now an adult, still remembers with excitement that celebration and his experiences throughout the year in Dad's classroom. Far from being turned off by it, Dad's students *wanted* to come to school each day.

For a while, Dad enjoyed a collection of live exotic pets. We had an albino skunk named Ralph that used to bounce around the house. He was harmless, but when strangers came over Ralph reared up on his haunches, hissed loudly, and attacked them. We had to give him up eventually when the biting got out of control.

We also had two boa constrictors—a nine-footer named Julius Squeezer, and a four-footer named Junior. During the school year, Dad kept the snakes in a large, heated terrarium in his classroom. He was absent one day and his substitute accidentally forgot to latch the top. Julius escaped that night. The following day someone noticed that Julius was missing. School was closed while wranglers from the Fish and Game Commission searched for him. They eventually found him coiled up in a heat register.

Another time, Dad brought Julius to my school to show the

students. While he was giving a lecture, he let the kids pass the snake around. One boy, Bob Menard, lifted Julius by the midsection instead of grabbing him right behind the head. Julius quickly turned and bit down on Bob's elbow. That snake must have had hundreds of teeth, because Bob bled profusely. Dad called Bob's parents to apologize and in the process met Bob's father, Curt Menard, the town dentist. Not long after that, we became Curt's patients and the two men became best friends.

Unfortunately, Julius and Junior met a tragic end. One night we placed a live rat in their cage for dinner. Unbeknownst to us, Julius and Junior both bit into the rat at the same time. Junior refused to let go, so Julius swallowed him and the rat at the same time. The next morning Julius had a strange, four-foot bulge in his body and we realized what had happened. Junior turned out to be more than Julius could handle. Julius died two days later.

We also had a large tarantula in our house. I never liked spiders, and this one was especially creepy. It often escaped from its cage at night and scared us all. After several episodes, Mom told Dad that if it happened again, she was going to get rid of the spider. Sure enough, it happened again and after the spider was returned to its cage, Mom placed the cage on the back porch. The temperature happened to be twenty degrees below zero that night so the spider didn't last long. All of these strange animals, plus our dog Rufus and Fifi the cat, made our house an interesting place for the neighborhood kids to hang out.

Dad's unconventional teaching methods proved very effective and they did exactly what he wanted. They inspired his students, including us, to a life of learning. His willingness to empower his students to fully experience the classroom subject matter involved a certain amount of risk—as with Bob Menard there was the real possibility of injury; a child might slip off the trail and fall, exposure to the cold might place a student in danger, or someone might get sick at the sight and smell of a live turkey being prepared for lunch. However, the benefit of Dad's approach more than made the risk worth taking. His teaching methods unleashed a sense of creativity unobtainable any other way. We were part of that process and learned not just the classroom subjects but a dynamic way of thinking. We also gained the confidence to work out our own solutions, to solve our own problems, and chart our own course.

Many people simply experience life, never taking the time to analyze events or think of how things could be different. Sarah was not like that. Even as a young girl she was an observer, and it carried over to her adult life. Juanita Fuller, one of Sarah's best friends, said, "Sarah is a thinker, an internal processor. She thinks her way through a situation."

Often that thought process takes her to a counterintuitive conclusion, which some have attacked as illogical or disingenuous. That's what they said when she proposed cutting property taxes in Wasilla as a way of stimulating growth. They repeated the same arguments when she suggested the city build a multiuse sports complex and pay for it with a sales-tax increase. In spite of opposition, both of those decisions proved to be great successes for the city and led to unprecedented growth.

Later, as governor, Sarah endured similar attacks when she proposed a solution to the Alaska gasline issue that excluded a sweetheart deal for the major petroleum companies. And the accusations continued when she confronted those same oil companies over their failure to develop oil fields on the North Slope. Everyone told her nontraditional, innovative approaches wouldn't work in government, that private companies wouldn't compete for construction of the gas line and she couldn't oust major oil companies from their leases. She proved them wrong on all counts and she did that by thinking her way through the problem to arrive at dynamic answers, using the same kind of unconventional methodology Dad used in his classroom.

That contrarian viewpoint, coupled with the courage to act on her conclusions, made her a serious threat to existing power structures within the state of Alaska, the Republican Party, and the permanent political class that controls the nation's capital. Her unconventional outlook made her unafraid to try something new. Rather than turning off voters—which was what traditional analysts said would happen—Sarah's fearless resourcefulness gave her broad appeal. Adrienne Ross, a teacher from Hudson, New York, put it this way: "One thing I respect about Governor Palin is her willingness to go out on a limb, even when others are playing it safe." Little did we know Sarah's nontraditional approach meant leaving the governor's office.

In the spring of 2009, Sarah attended the Alyeska Spring Carnival and Slush Cup. It's an event held every spring at Alyeska Ski Resort, about thirty miles south of Anchorage, and marks the end of the winter ski season. It comes at a time when, as the name implies, the snow has turned to slush. Costumed skiers and snowboarders speed down the slope and try to skim across a ninety-foot pool of water at the bottom of the run. Contestants are judged on their costume, how much air they catch coming off the slope, the kind of tricks they perform, and how far they make it across the pond. It's a big event and very popular. Sarah was there as an honorary judge.

Todd and the children accompanied Sarah to the event and stayed with her at the hotel. I was there with my family too. After the event, I went up to Sarah's room and we talked alone for a while. In the months that followed the 2008 presidential campaign, a number of frivolous ethics charges had been filed against her. At times it seemed like there was a new one every week. I knew it was wearing on her, and we all knew it was taking a heavy financial toll on her family. Filing an ethics complaint costs nothing, but at the time an official made the target of such a charge was required to defend that case at his or her own expense. By law, the state was prohibited from covering Sarah's legal expenses.

That night Sarah and I discussed the situation. The steady drip, drip, drip of complaints weighed heavily on her and I asked how much more she could take. She said she didn't know, but the time, money, and resources expended on her defense were crippling her administration and making her governorship much less effective. Many members of her staff were spending up to 90 percent of their workday dealing with the complaints—valuable time that should have been used to handle state business. This was the first time that I'd ever heard Sarah voice such frustration.

Sarah never gave me any indication that night that she would be making the decision to step down in a few short months, but I wondered how it was going to work out and whether events could come to a happy conclusion. It didn't help matters to have local newspapers working to sensationalize the claims contained in the complaints.

On the morning of July 3, the day she made the announcement to step down, I received a phone call from Todd asking me to be at their house later that day for an important announcement. He didn't share any further details and I had no idea what was about to happen.

At the appointed hour, I gathered with our extended family on the lawn at Sarah's home. Behind us, the water of Lake Lucille shimmered in the bright summer sun beneath a cloudless sky. Ducks floated serenely just a few feet from shore. We stood in a line that formed to the left and right behind the podium, waiting to hear what Sarah would say. A large contingent of reporters and cameramen gathered there too, and were arrayed in front of us.

Sarah appeared and in a few minutes she stepped toward the podium. As she did, she leaned close to me and whispered in my ear, "Say a prayer for me." My mind raced as I struggled to understand what she meant. The conversation we'd had earlier that spring never crossed my mind. All I could think of was an announcement about a new gasline deal or something like that. Minutes later, when she looked into the cameras and said that she was stepping down, my jaw dropped. Mom and Dad were standing beside me. All I could say was, "Wow." We all were stunned.

Though we were caught off guard by the announcement, we knew firsthand how reckless and out of control the ethics complaints had become. From the time Sarah became governor until the day she was announced as John McCain's running mate, the governor's office received forty-nine requests for public disclosure of government records. Most of them were handled in a routine manner. At that same time, there were only three ethics complaints pending against her. In Alaska politics, ethics complaints are a favorite tool of those opposing whomever is in office and are regularly used by both parties to bring claims against each other. That three complaints had been filed against her was nothing new. Those three complaints were all dismissed in routine fashion.

After she was announced as the Republican Party's vice presidential candidate, things changed dramatically. Within days, additional requests for records disclosures poured in, very quickly reaching a total of 189. Ethics complaints rose too. Four days after she was announced as McCain's running mate, she filed a self-disclosure complaint regarding matters raised in the dispute with Walt Monegan that became known as Troopergate—the allegation that Sarah had used her position as governor in an attempt to force Monegan to fire an Alaska State Trooper. Then, from September 2008 through April 2009, fourteen additional complaints were filed against her. A number of those complaints were patently frivolous and were dismissed out of hand, but three claims remained unresolved at the time she resigned. The state had incurred almost two million dollars in expenses related to handling the ethics claims, most of it in the form of lost employee time.

By traditional analysis, the claims against her represented the fight of her life. For many, particularly those who viewed government from a politics-as-usual perspective, Sarah's political future was on the line and with it any hope she had of capitalizing on the goodwill she'd accrued during the 2008 campaign. But that was not how Sarah saw it. For her, it was a fight for the state and one she could not win by traditional means. Remaining in office and defending those ethics charges as a sitting public official would accomplish nothing except the defense of her own reputation. For her, that was unacceptable. She wasn't interested in using her office merely as a means of defending against the charges. So she resigned.

In the days following her resignation, many concluded that she left office to pursue lucrative opportunities in the private sector. As Reid Smith, her former coach, observed, "They didn't understand that Sarah really had the interests of Alaska in mind." It's easy to see why people might reach that conclusion—money permeates our society and many people would have chosen the money over service if they'd been faced with the same decision. With Sarah, nothing could have been further from the truth. For her, the choice to leave office was always about what was best for the people of Alaska. She didn't run from the fight, she merely chose to pursue it by other means.

The fact that drilling won't solve every problem is no excuse to do nothing at all.

Sarah Palin

〜

CHAPTER 12

Oil

*The struggle to free the state from the clutches of those
powerful forces became a battle that defined Sarah
as a politician.*
CHUCK HEATH SR.

Two years after the conclusion of the Civil War, William H. Seward, the US secretary of state, negotiated the purchase of Alaska from the Russian Empire. The treaty containing terms of the purchase was signed on March 30, 1867, and approved by the Senate the following month. Another year passed before Congress appropriated the money to conclude the sale. Labeled "Seward's Folly" by those who opposed the purchase, it proved to be the greatest acquisition since the Louisiana Purchase and the sole accomplishment of Andrew Johnson's beleaguered term as US president.

Earlier attempts to acquire the land had been delayed by the onset of the Civil War, then mired in the political conflict that swirled around Johnson's presidency. Even after approval of the acquisition, Congressional appropriation of the money to fund the purchase was delayed by Johnson's impeachment and subsequent trial. It was an inauspicious beginning for such a magnificent tract of land, one that foreshadowed the struggle to come as the true value that lay beneath Alaska's wilderness came to light.

For the sixty years following the purchase, Alaska passed through various forms of federal administration until it was officially organized as a territory in 1912. Almost immediately, civic leaders began working toward its full admission to the Union as the nation's forty-ninth state. James Wickersham, one of Alaska's first territorial delegates to Congress, led the fight. He died in 1930, without achieving the statehood goal, but by then the idea had become a cause championed by many throughout the territory.

The move toward statehood continued to gain momentum and in 1949, the Alaska Territorial Legislature established a Statehood Committee charged with conducting the research and preliminary deliberations necessary for creating a state government. Following a territory-wide referendum on the issue, delegates from across the land gathered on November 8, 1955, in Fairbanks, and began the work of writing what would become the state's first constitution. When Sarah became governor, she honored those founders by holding her inauguration in the same room where they drafted that document fifty years before.

Unlike other state constitutions, the constitution of Alaska includes a specific article addressing use and development of the state's natural resources. That provision, made necessary by the terms of federal legislation granting statehood, prohibited the state from disposing of mineral interests in land granted to the state and made state-owned natural resources in Alaska a public domain to be used, conserved, and developed for the betterment of its citizens. That article was put to its first real test in the 1970s.

From prehistoric times, native Alaskans had been aware of naturally occurring oil seepages at various locations around the state. Early Russian explorers and settlers noted oil seeping from the ground on the southwestern Alaska Peninsula but made no attempt to exploit it. In the 1890s, the first oil wells were drilled on the western shore of Cook Inlet. However, oil from those wells was mixed with seawater and the venture proved unprofitable. In 1911, several wells were drilled on the Copper River delta. Some of them produced significant amounts of oil, which was refined in a place called Katalla and shipped to Cordova for distribution.

Then, in 1957, the Richfield Oil Company of California discovered a major oil field on the Kenai Peninsula. The discovery of that field prompted an "oil rush" as companies covered the state in search of oil. Ten years later they found what they were looking for at Prudhoe Bay, an icy inlet on Alaska's northern coast. Test wells drilled in the surrounding area confirmed the northern slope of the Brooks Range, an area stretching from the Brooks Mountains to the Arctic Ocean and covering more than 213,000 acres, held an estimated twenty-five billion barrels of oil. It was the largest deposit of oil on the North American continent. All that remained was an efficient way to get that oil to market. For the oil companies, the only workable solution was a pipeline.

What they proposed was not a new idea. Pipelines had been built in Alaska and Canada before. During World War II, the demand for oil skyrocketed. The US and Canadian governments worked together to construct a line four inches in diameter that stretched from oil fields in Canada's Northwest Territories to the Tank Farm in Skagway. The amount of oil flowing through that line wasn't significant by today's terms but it proved that a pipeline could be constructed in a region filled with daunting physical obstacles and extreme weather conditions. It could be done, but the scale necessary to exploit the Prudhoe Bay field was staggering.

After careful deliberation, the oil companies chose a trans-Alaska route for the pipeline that traversed the entire state, from Prudhoe Bay in the north to the city of Valdez on Prince William Sound in the south.

For marketing oil, the pipeline was a good idea, but it faced several formidable obstacles. One of the biggest hurdles was the intrusion the pipeline would make over traditional native Alaskan lands.

At the time oil was discovered on Prudhoe Bay, most of interior Alaska remained unsettled except for areas occupied by native Alaskans in their traditional villages. In spite of Alaska's rise to statehood, aboriginal claims to those lands remained unresolved. Most villages and communities exercised physical control over specific areas as the resource for their subsistence lifestyle, but the issue of legal title to the land had never been concluded. The proposed pipeline route bisected many of those traditional areas. Objections to its construction prompted many of those native groups to file lawsuits seeking to halt the project.

After intense negotiations, native objections were resolved by Congress in 1971, with the passage of the Alaska Native Claims Settlement Act. That act gave specific native cultural groups large cash settlements and ownership of expansive tracts of land that encompassed native settlements and traditional hunting grounds. As part of that settlement, native groups dropped their opposition to construction of the pipeline.

Environmentalists, who were convinced that a pipeline would destroy Alaska's ecology, posed a second obstacle. They joined the fight against the project and obtained an injunction to halt its construction. The oil companies worked hard to develop a plan that addressed environmental concerns, but the two sides were far apart. Then, with a worldwide oil crisis looming on the horizon, Alaska's congressional delegation and prominent federal officials moved the debate to Congress. In 1973, the Alaska Pipeline Authorization Act was approved, with Vice President Spiro Agnew casting the deciding vote in the Senate.

Finally, with native claims settled and environmental objections trumped by Congress, oil companies turned to the lone remaining obstacle—the engineering challenges posed by building something so big in a land so inhospitable. To reach Prince William Sound, the pipeline had to cut an eight-hundred-mile swath through some of the toughest terrain on earth—including tundra on the North Slope, three major mountain ranges, and numerous rivers.

Construction began in the winter of 1973, and oil was flowing by the summer of 1977. Twenty-eight thousand people were employed on the construction project and the final cost was estimated to be eight billion dollars, making it the largest privately funded construction project of its day. At peak production, approximately two million barrels of oil per day flowed through the pipeline to ships and holding facilities at the terminal in Valdez, supplying almost 25 percent of America's domestic oil.

As oil flowed through the pipeline, Gov. Jay Hammond proposed an amendment to the state constitution designating that a portion of the state's oil revenue be placed into an account to be shared with all Alaskans. This was the beginning of the Alaska Permanent Fund. In 1982, every Alaskan resident received a check for $1,000. Sarah, who was still a minor, received two. Sally mailed one of them back and called the state agency to tell them there was a mistake. A week later, Sarah got a third check in the mail. Rather than return it, Sally voided that one and it now hangs on the wall of our garage as a memento.

Construction of the pipeline, and the oil that flowed through it, had little immediate effect on the price of oil, but it had a tremendous effect on Alaska. It changed Wasilla, too. Located near the edge of Anchorage's suburban sprawl, Wasilla provided a convenient staging point for construction crews working the southern half of the pipeline. The town saw a dramatic increase in population.

Revenue from exploitation of the North Slope field serviced by the pipeline later provided infrastructure and conveniences many towns had never seen. It also made us dependent on oil and led to widespread corruption. In the process, Alaska lost some of its frontier innocence. As our friend Elsie O'Brien said, "Everyone up here is just people, especially in the old days." That was true before the pipeline. After that, everything started to change.

Many of the changes were simply the result of money. Income from development of the oil fields meant oil companies had the resources to pay workers at rates far above what they could earn anywhere else. High wages attracted potential employees from other parts of the country. It also put more money in the hands of Alaska's citizens, who were among the many with oil-industry jobs. Sarah's husband, Todd, hired on with BP for work on the Slope. The money he earned didn't make them rich, but it was enough to provide a comfortable life. Many other Alaskans obtained jobs in the industry and the money they earned went right into the local economy.

More money meant more buying power, which created waves of economic activity still being felt today. Revenue from increased business provided towns and boroughs with resources to upgrade government services and infrastructure. Much of what Sarah was able to accomplish as mayor of Wasilla came from the increased economic activity made possible by revenue from the oil industry as that revenue worked its way through the economy. State revenue, taken in the form of taxes on production, allowed the state to forego the imposition of a state income tax.

At the same time, changes occurred that were not so good. Oil companies developed cozy relationships with Alaska officials. Contributions from major oil companies flowed into the campaign accounts of elected officials charged by the state constitution with protecting, preserving, and administering the state's natural resources. Boundaries between the companies and regulators were often blurred. In that environment, a culture of corruption flourished.

Then, on March 24, 1989, the *Exxon Valdez* struck Bligh Reef in Prince William Sound. The impact of the collision ripped a hole in the hull of the tanker and Alaskan crude poured into the water. Within hours, the Sound's pristine ecological system was in serious danger. The environmental nightmare many conservation groups predicted came true, only the culprit wasn't the Trans-Alaska Pipeline or drilling crews on the North Slope. The problem came from human error. According to testimony offered during the several trials that followed, the captain of the ship was asleep. The ship was in the hands of its third mate. He would have made it safely out to sea if the ship's radar had been working. It wasn't, and apparently hadn't been for at least a year.

Damage to Prince William Sound, and collateral damage to the Alaska seafood industry, told Alaskans what they already knew—extraction of oil was a dangerous business. Alaska is beautiful, but that beauty can be deceptive and in an unguarded moment the awful power behind that beauty can become deadly.

Most of us knew the risk of developing the state's oil and gas resources and understood that without diligent attention to proper care, the industry that brought great wealth to our state could become an instrument of great destruction. What we didn't count on was the way oil companies would react to an environmental problem. The *Exxon Valdez* oil spill opened our eyes.

Conservative estimates suggested eleven million gallons of oil escaped from the ship. Some environmental groups place the amount at thirty-two million. Regardless of the exact numbers, the spill was one of history's largest man made environmental disasters. Thousands of birds and shoreline animals died as a result. Alaska's seafood industry was dealt a devastating blow. Prices for salmon and other fresh fish plummeted as buyers avoided the market. Fish from other inlets and bays were unaffected by the spill but none of that mattered. No one wanted to buy Alaskan seafood. Litigation began almost immediately.

Todd and Sarah fished the commercial salmon season at Bristol Bay. Reporters have suggested their fishing business wasn't a significant endeavor. As I noted earlier, I worked the boats with them during that period and I saw firsthand how hard they both worked. Income from fishing provided a substantial portion of their livelihood. Losing it to the oil spill struck a heavy financial blow.

In the aftermath of the spill, the oil company launched an extensive publicity campaign in an attempt to showcase efforts to clean up the oil, blunt the effect of pending litigation, and win public approval for its handling of the situation. Many in the region found jobs on cleanup crews. The hours were long but the pay was good. Molly, Chuck Jr., and I worked on a crew that summer after the academic year ended at school. We returned the following summer as part of a final cleanup push. Some of the remediation efforts helped—cleaning wildlife and skimming oil off the Sound. Quite a lot of it was ineffective and some made the situation worse.

In the initial weeks after the spill, chemical dispersant was sprayed on the oil slick in an effort to break up the heavy crude. That dispersant was soon found to be harmful to crews working the shoreline and toxic to wildlife. One of the more publicized efforts used steam in an attempt to blast the oil from the rocky coastline. Industry experts suggested the oil would then wash back into the Sound, where skimmers could collect it. Some of the oil along the shoreline was collected in this manner. More of it was driven deeper into the ground, only to emerge later.

Meanwhile, litigation dragged into the mid-1990s, when a jury finally issued a verdict against Exxon. The company appealed and the legal process continued, ultimately lasting decades. Final payment of amounts awarded to those damaged by the oil did not come until 2010, twenty years after the spill.

In the years prior to the *Exxon Valdez* disaster, many were of the opinion that "what's good for the oil companies is good for Alaska." By the time litigation over the spill ended, empathy for the oil companies was long since gone and the culture of self-interest that developed in state government became visible to everyone. Sarah confronted that culture in 2003, when she served as chairperson of the state Oil and Gas Conservation Commission. At the time, Randy Ruedrich, an oil and gas commissioner, was also chairman of the state Republican Party. Sarah saw a conflict of interest in his efforts to obtain party campaign donations from executives of oil companies whose businesses were regulated by the commission. Her allegations and attempts to address the situation placed her in direct conflict with the state Republican Party and the long standing network of alliances between elected officials and oil-company executives—alliances that spanned both political parties.

Later, after leaving the commission, she joined with Eric Croft, a Democrat, in raising claims that the state attorney general had a similar conflict of interest by reason of stock he owned in a company with which the governor's office was negotiating a coal export agreement—negotiations that he was leading. As governor, she once again confronted entrenched opposition when she moved forward with attempts to force oil companies to develop their leases at Point Thomson and when she began work toward developing a new pipeline to bring natural gas from the North Slope to the lower forty-eight states.

The forces Sarah confronted were more than mere ideological antagonism from an opposing political party. The forces she faced were formidable and historic in nature. They didn't arise merely to oppose her in typical political fashion. They arose from a power structure fifty years in the making—a structure developed to influence the institutions of state government in a manner most advantageous to those who sought to exploit the state's natural resources, without regard for the benefit that exploitation might provide to the state's citizens. The struggle to free the state from the clutches of those powerful forces became a battle that defined Sarah as a politician.

If character is the measure in this election, and hope the theme, and change the goal we share, then I ask you to join our cause.

Sarah Palin

CHAPTER 13

College

*From an early age, our parents instilled in us a love of
learning. They were lifelong learners and we grew up
immersed in their intellectual curiosity.*
CHUCK HEATH JR.

W hen Sarah was nominated as John McCain's running
mate for the 2008 presidential campaign, news reporters seized on several trivial issues from her past. One of the first
things they jumped on was her college record. Reporters were
quick to note that she'd attended multiple colleges before graduating. None of them got the story correct and none of it really
mattered anyway, but it was aggravating to see them focus on
something so inconsequential. A recent study indicated that as
many as one-third of all college seniors transferred at least once.
Every time the issue comes up at an event or in conversation, any
number of people respond with their own stories about the multiple schools at which they studied, often without ever obtaining
a degree. Sarah, on the other hand, graduated with a bachelor's
degree in journalism and she paid for it with her own money.

From an early age, our parents instilled in us a love of learning. They were lifelong learners and we grew up immersed in their
intellectual curiosity. Visitors who stop by their house marvel at

the animal trophy heads that line the walls of their home. Goat, sheep, and caribou ring the space above the windows in the family room. Animal skins from every fur-bearing Alaskan animal drape the banister from the second floor. Downstairs, in the basement, shelves that line the walls are filled with the skulls of more animals. If you sit long enough to drink a cup of coffee with Dad, he'll drag out a folder of photographs and tell you stories about the hunt that brought those animals to the house. He went on as many hunts with a camera as he did with a rifle.

Every animal we killed came to the house for two purposes— as meat for the freezer and a lesson in biology and zoology. We received lecture after lecture about how the animals hunted and foraged, what they ate, and how their bodies digested their food, along with an exposition about their migratory patterns and how the ones that stayed up north learned techniques that allowed them to survive the harsh Alaskan winters.

Both our parents were lifelong learners, so not attending college was never an option for us and we never once considered doing anything else. The catch for us was that we had to pay for it ourselves.

Some parents provide a college education for their children. I hope I can pay for my children to attend a college of their choice, but my sisters and I had to figure out how to pay for it as we went. We all took loans of one form or another and worked, but having to finance it ourselves influenced our choices of what colleges to attend. Expensive schools really were not an option. The other thing that influenced our choice was distance.

Alaska has three major cities—Juneau, Fairbanks, and Anchorage. It's the largest state in the union by landmass, but one of the smallest states by population. We have one major university with classes conducted in three locations. If you go to college in Alaska your options are cold, colder, and coldest. If you want to go outside the state, the nearest schools are in the states of Washington, Idaho, and Montana. The drive from Wasilla to Pullman, Washington, home of Washington State University, covers 2,400 miles. The drive to the University of Idaho, in Moscow, Idaho, is roughly the same distance. The University of Montana is in Missoula, Montana, 2,500 miles from our home. Traveling from our home in Alaska, to make the traditional college road trip students in the lower forty-eight states take as a way of visiting campuses during their senior year in high school, was out of the question. A trip like that would take a week and cover 5,000 miles—just to drive to one out-of-state campus, turn around, and come back. In the 1980s, the expense of a trip like that would go a long way toward paying the first semester's tuition. We had to forego the road trip and choose a college based on admissions brochures, catalogs, and word of mouth.

Eventually, my sisters and I ended up at schools in Idaho. Our grandparents from both sides of the family lived nearby and we had visited there often as children. Various relatives and friends had attended one or the other of the schools we ultimately chose, so we knew a little of what to expect. We also knew what to expect from the area in general and enjoyed the region. Before she made that final choice, however, Sarah wanted to try Hawaii.

When we were younger—I was fifteen or sixteen—our aunt Katie lived near Waikiki. One year, our mother offered us a chance to fly out there for a visit. There was one caveat, however. Like everything else we wanted, we had to pay our own way. We made a huge calendar and began marking off the dates in anticipation of our departure, and we went to work earning the money to pay for the airline tickets for the trip out there. I don't remember how much it cost, but I do remember we all worked and saved to make it happen. The sand, surf, and sunshine were quite a contrast to life in Alaska, and Aunt Katie made sure we had fun. That trip made an indelible impression on Sarah. When it came time to choose a college, she wanted to give Hawaii a try. She was paying for it. She could go anywhere she could afford. Our friend Kim Ketchum and three other girls from Wasilla joined her.

They applied for admission to the University of Hawaii and were admitted to a campus in Hilo. With visions of the waves and beaches from our childhood dancing in their heads, they set out for a freshman year of sun and fun. When they arrived, they found Hilo soaked in damp, rainy weather, apparently the norm for that location. Midway through orientation they asked to be reassigned to the campus in Honolulu, but there was no room. Instead, they arranged a transfer to Hawaii Pacific College, not far from where our aunt Katie lived.

After a semester of study, they had reached their limit of eighty-degree, sunshine-filled days. As Christmas approached they began to realize how much they missed living in a region that experienced distinctive seasons. Christmas in shorts and T-shirts just wasn't how they were made. Over the midyear break, they transferred to North Idaho College, a community college located in Coeur d'Alene. The campus was about an hour south of Sandpoint, the town where Sarah had been born. I had gone there myself.

During my senior year in high school I was selected for an honorable mention on the *Parade Magazine* high school All-American team. College recruiters came to see me play and courted me with the possibility of a major college scholarship. They pursued me right up to the time I broke my leg. I had planned on going to college in Oregon with a football scholarship but after I was injured the recruiters vanished. Recovery took a while, but eventually I returned to sports.

While playing baseball in an American Legion tournament, Jack Bloxom, the head coach at North Idaho College, approached me about playing baseball for him. I didn't have a lot of other options, so that fall I packed my bags and headed to Idaho. My baseball career didn't amount to much; I was a second-string catcher behind an excellent player who later signed a contract with the New York Mets, but athletics got me partway to a degree.

For the remainder of my college education I attended the University of Idaho. The campus was exactly what I'd always envisioned a university should be—ivy-covered walls, beautiful redbrick buildings, and a classic Greek fraternity row. My grandmother, Helen Sheeran, had lived on that same Greek row when she attended the university in the 1920s. I pledged Sigma Alpha Epsilon. Our house was right down the street from the one where Helen had lived.

Shortly after arriving on campus, I tried out for the football team as a "walk-on"—a nonscholarship player who simply shows up and hopes for a spot on the roster. Joining the team as a nonrecruited player was a humbling experience for me. Most of the players had been sought out by team scouts and provided with scholarships, a fact they never tired of telling me. The first person on the team whom I met was a defensive lineman named Frank Moreno. I made the mistake of telling him about the *Parade Magazine* honorable mention. In practice, Frank made a point of hitting me on every play and then said with a sneer, "How's it going, All-American?"

Eventually we became friends and he was my "Big Brother" at the fraternity. Frank and I both majored in elementary education. He was fluent in Spanish, however, and was recruited by the Drug Enforcement Agency (DEA) to work as an undercover agent. With long hair and an ever-present scowl he had no trouble playing the part of a drug dealer. A few years later, Frank was shot and killed while on assignment in Colombia.

As the first season began, I was listed as number seven on the depth chart at running back. Many of the players ahead of me were faster than I was, but in every practice I ran like my life depended on it. When our first game arrived, I was still well down in the playing order. As we stood in the tunnel ready to charge onto the field, I heard a voice yelling down from above, "Go get 'em, Chucky!" I looked up and saw my high school principal, Ed Frandsen, looking down at me. He had flown all the way down to watch my first game.

College life kept me busy. I carried a full load of classes, worked as a dishwasher at a sorority, and played football. I had never really been one to party in high school, and neither had my sisters. We were too worried about jeopardizing our athletic and academic careers, and we knew Mom and Dad wouldn't approve of it. After our high school graduation ceremonies, we celebrated with members from our church youth group at a bowling alley. College was a different matter, at least for me. Free of parental constraints, I attended too many parties and my GPA slipped below 2.0. I was placed on academic probation and had to plead with the dean for my academic life. I used the excuse that my busy schedule was interfering with my studies, which was only partially true. When I got home that summer and Dad saw my grades, he straightened out my priorities.

After finishing her freshman year at North Idaho College, Sarah came home for the summer. That's when Linda Menard convinced Sarah to enter the Miss Wasilla pageant. Linda and her husband, Curt, had been influential throughout our lives. They were good friends with our parents and mentors to us, encouraging us to reach for goals that often seemed beyond our grasp.

Curt was our dentist. He treated us in exchange for firewood and often accompanied Dad on his trips to the mountains. When we were in elementary school, Curt injured his right arm in an electrical accident and the arm had to be amputated. He was right-handed and many thought it was the end of his dental career—everyone except Curt. Not long after the surgery Dad paid him a visit. Instead of finding him depressed and forlorn, Curt was propped up in bed practicing fine motor skills with his left hand. When he returned to his dental practice, Dad volunteered as one of Curt's first patients. Curt went on to a long career not only as a dentist but as mayor of Mat-Su Borough and as a member of the Alaska legislature.

Linda and Curt came to Alaska from Michigan, where Linda had been involved in beauty pageants. After they moved to Alaska she continued her involvement with pageants and owned the Alaska franchise for Mrs. America. Asked why she encouraged Sarah to enter the Miss Wasilla competition, Linda said simply, "I saw something in her." Curt saw something too. He used to say, "I don't know where that girl's going, but she's going somewhere."

We all saw something in her. We just never saw her as a "pageant girl." She was an athlete and not the least bit interested in the things women must do to win beauty competitions, but Linda would not be deterred and finally hit on the one selling point that caught Sarah's attention: scholarships. If she won even a single segment of the competition she could win a college scholarship. Linda worked with her and gave her tips and help in preparing for the event. She remembered Sarah "was not inclined toward labels," which made it difficult to convince her of the need to wear the dresses Linda knew were necessary for pageant competition.

On the night of the pageant we were all nervous for her. I wasn't worried about whether Sarah would win. I just didn't want her to embarrass herself. Our friend Adrian Lane said the other day, "Everyone underestimates Sarah." We sure underestimated her that night. She won the Miss Wasilla competition hands down and took every segment of the event. Geraldine Ferraro was the vice presidential candidate for the Democratic Party that year and the judges asked Sarah if she thought a woman could serve as vice president. "Yes," she answered. "I think a woman could be vice president. I think a woman could be president."

Winning the local competition qualified Sarah for the Miss Alaska pageant. She earned second runner-up in that event and also won the title of Miss Congeniality. Scholarships from those two pageants were a big help in paying for her remaining years in school. With that assistance, she moved on from North Idaho and joined me at the University of Idaho.

During my senior year of college, I lived in an apartment. Sarah and her roommate, Ana de la Cueva, came by occasionally to hang out, but they were both busy. Ana was from Guadalajara, Mexico, and was in school on a tennis scholarship. Most days she was either in class or at practice. Sarah was very serious about school and wasn't really into the social scene at all. She attended parties occasionally but I never saw her drink. Unlike me, she was very goal oriented and refused to participate in anything that might sidetrack her from attaining those goals.

While we were in college in Idaho, our cousin Greg Jones attended Washington State University just a few miles away in Pullman, Washington. He spent much of his time playing with a band. When he wasn't with them, he was at the fraternity house with me. As I indicated earlier, I had too much fun in college and Greg enjoyed most of it with me. He remembered Sarah during those days as a quiet, conservative student. "Her main job was to look at Chuck and me and tell us what pigs we were." We could get a little crazy at times, but Sarah was pretty straitlaced. She and her friends spent occasional weekends in Spokane, shopping and hanging out. Most of the time, however, she was in her room studying, or talking on the phone to Todd. They were already serious about their relationship.

The year after I graduated, Sarah stayed at home and attended Mat-Su Community College. She returned to the University of Idaho a year later and graduated in 1987. That brings me to the other issue reporters repeatedly attacked—the fact that she attended a state school as opposed to a prestigious private school on the East Coast. It is true that most presidents and vice presidents who obtained an undergraduate degree did so from private colleges. However, millions of Americans—including Vice President Joe Biden—got their post-secondary education from publicly funded universities.

For some, college is an eye-opening experience, a time of self-awakening and self-discovery. For Sarah, it was simply the next step toward a career she thought would include sports journalism. Self-discovery came to her in stages but college wasn't really one of them. She had a clear sense of purpose and vision long before she graduated from high school. If there was an epiphany moment in her teenage years, it came with basketball at Wasilla High School when she learned that, with hard work and determination, she really could accomplish more than others thought possible. Her sense of self developed further when she won a seat on the Wasilla City Council and continued to grow as she moved forward in politics. College, which fell in between high school and a political career, was more a time of maturation than anything else. For the first time in her life, she had the opportunity to see herself outside the context of our tightly woven family. I think she liked what she saw.

People know something has gone terribly wrong with our government and it has gotten so far off track. But people also know that there is nothing wrong in America that a good old-fashioned election can't fix.

Sarah Palin

CHAPTER 14

Politics

As she already knew, those volunteers
turned out to be as good as gold.
CHUCK HEATH SR.

If you came to our house when the kids were young, you would
have heard a discussion about the latest hunting trip, or the
hunting trip we were planning, or yet one more version of something that happened on the trail—like the time Chuck Jr. got
stuck on the mountain and couldn't get down. You might encounter a very animated debate about the latest high school sporting
event or about teams in the NFL, or the NHL, or the NBA. But
until Sarah ran for a seat on the Wasilla City Council, you never
would have heard an impassioned discussion about politics.

We weren't apolitical—we talked among ourselves about the
Watergate hearings, President Nixon's resignation, and the fact
that President Ford played football in college and declined an
offer to turn pro, opting instead for law school and a career in
politics. In the late seventies, everyone in town had an opinion
about President Carter. When he took office, we were hit with
double-digit inflation, then his administration created seventeen
new national monuments. That decision alone closed some fifty-
six million acres of federal land in Alaska to gold mining, timber

harvesting, and other operations. The federal government still owned 60 percent of Alaska, which meant those land-use changes put many Alaskans out of business. In Fairbanks, enraged Alaskans burned Carter in effigy and picketed outside the US Post Office. Bumper stickers appeared with slogans like, WE DON'T GIVE A DAMN HOW THEY DO IT OUTSIDE! There are many living here who remain furious with Carter and his policies.

In spite of that, political discussions at our house never reached the level of intensity we gave to sports, hunting, or outdoor activities. There were political strains running through our family—Clem Sheeran, Sally's father, was involved in politics; my father had felt a patriotic duty during World War II; and I had served in the Army—but for the most part, as a family, we paid those influences scant attention. I was busy teaching and hunting. Sally was busy keeping us straight and making sure everyone got where they needed to go. Chuck Jr. was interested in football, Heather excelled at basketball, and Molly was good at everything. Yet all the while, those historic family political influences, faint though they may have been, found a place in Sarah. Among those historic strains, Clem influenced her the most.

Born in Waterville, Washington, he attended Columbia University (now the University of Portland) in Portland, Oregon, where he played football and ran track. He was there two years and then transferred to Idaho State University, in Pocatello. While there, he was asked to join Helen Gower, a fellow student at the university, to sing at the wedding of a mutual friend. They struck up a friendship that grew into love and were married. Helen was Sally's mother and the grandmother of our children.

Clem and Helen spent their early years together in Salt Lake City, where he worked for DuPont. They had four children then (two more would come later) and lived an active life. He was handsome and cut an impressive figure. So impressive, he once was mistaken for the notorious bank robber Charles "Pretty Boy" Floyd. He sat in the Salt Lake City jail for a few hours until a friend came along who could vouch for his true identity.

In 1943, Clem was hired to work at the Hanford Nuclear Facility. Located near Richland, Washington, a small town along the Columbia River, Hanford was part of the government's Manhattan Project, the research and development effort that produced the atomic bomb. Reactors at the Hanford site produced weapons-grade plutonium used in "Fat Boy," the atomic bomb that was dropped on Nagasaki, Japan, near the close of World War II.

Originally hired to work in the warehouse, Clem distinguished himself very early as an advocate for employee rights. He had a clear sense of right and wrong and wasn't afraid to challenge management policies. An otherwise affable and congenial man, his fellow employees found him always willing to listen to their problems and equally ready to advance their cause. He taught himself labor law and developed a reputation as an expert in the field. A few years after arriving at Hanford he was promoted to personnel manager and spent the remainder of his career fighting for better working conditions for employees.

For most of his life he was active in sports—primarily tennis, softball, and golf—and participated in an amateur theater group. He was a referee for high school football games and took an active interest in the school his children attended. He also was interested in the life of the community and didn't mind taking the lead in a civic fight. The first of those fights came in 1962.

During the 1950s the Tri-Cities area—comprised of Richland, Kennewick, and Pasco—was home to a minor-league baseball team called the Tri-City Braves. In their first two seasons, the team drew large crowds and enjoyed the enthusiastic support of an active fan base. However, as the decade wore on, the team's performance diminished and so did the crowds. In 1962, the owners of the team ceased fielding a squad, abandoned the franchise, and allowed rights to the team to return to the league. When Clem heard about it, he insisted that something be done to keep the team active. He organized a group of investors who put up $500 each and created a fund that they used to obtain the franchise. Working together, they reorganized the team, which continued to play in Richland through the 1980s.

At the same time, school-board budget cuts led to a fight over funding for the high school athletic program. The board wanted to eliminate most sports. Clem led the effort to restore funding and organized a booster club for the high school that worked to improve athletic facilities. Part of that effort included a fund-raising basketball game with the Harlem Globetrotters. Students from the 1950s and 1960s still talk about that game. With Clem's leadership, the athletics program not only survived but flourished.

In 1967, Clem and others in the area became concerned about opposition to the Vietnam War and the effect antiwar protests might have on those serving in the US military. To address the issue, they organized the Tri-Cities Armed Services Committee and published a newsletter, which they distributed to men and women from the area serving in the military. The following year, Clem was elected chairman of the group and served two terms.

As 1970 arrived, Clem joined the fight to retain the city's embattled city manager. He also helped form the Richland Chamber of Commerce. Involvement in the life of the community opened his eyes to the need for good city government and, in 1971, he ran for a seat on the Richland City Council.

In typical Clem fashion he decided that he didn't need

contributions from donors or help from volunteers. Instead, he chose to finance the campaign himself. By refusing contributions, he would be free to govern without obligation to any special groups. He wanted to simply represent the people. He and his youngest son, Mike, prepared hand-lettered signs in the basement and posted them around town. That September, a nonpartisan primary election nominated him as one of two candidates for a council seat from his district, but he was defeated in the general election.

Not one to sit and watch, he organized a group of 1,600 former General Electric employees from Hanford to fight for pension benefits that had been granted by the company to other retirees but denied to those who worked at Hanford. Clem was elected chairman of a steering committee that shepherded their cause through the claims process. Working tirelessly to right what he perceived as an injustice, he raised money for legal fees, hired attorneys, and oversaw the resulting litigation. Doing that occupied much of his time for the next ten years. After a long fight, they reached an agreement that gave retirees a substantial increase in pension payments—not as much as they expected, but an increase just the same.

By 1982, Clem was seventy-five years old. Most men his age spent their days on the golf course or sitting at the café drinking coffee. Clem played golf and I'm certain he made his regular trips to the Spudnut doughnut shop, but he also kept an eye on events in Richland. When he heard about a pending deal to destroy his favorite golf course and develop most of the property into a shopping mall, he was incensed. The course was located near the entrance to Richland and offered a beautifully landscaped introduction to visitors. Replacing it with commercial buildings and a paved parking lot struck him as ludicrous.

When an initial inquiry into the matter raised his suspicions about how the deal was arranged, he joined in a fight to save the course. Later that year, he and four others were named plaintiffs in a class-action lawsuit over construction of the shopping center. Like the General Electric litigation, the fate of the golf course lingered unresolved for ten years. In the end, Clem successfully reached a compromise that allowed the golf course to remain, alongside a smaller, scaled-down version of the retail development.

In his later years, Clem suffered from macular degeneration and his eyesight quickly deteriorated. At first he denied there was a problem and did his best to hide the seriousness of the condition. He had been a high school football referee for years but in one of his last games he dropped the coin at the coin toss. The coin lay in the grass at his feet but he couldn't see it and had to ask one of the players to retrieve it. Not long after that, he gave up refereeing.

He continued to drive for a few more years until the day he rear-ended a potato truck. When the policeman arrived at the scene, he asked Clem if he'd been drinking or taking drugs. Clem said no. Then the policeman asked if he had even seen the truck at all. Clem had to admit that he hadn't seen it and he realized he'd reached the end of his driving career.

In 1992, we received a call telling us that Clem was in the last stages of his final fight, a battle with pancreatic cancer. Sally and Chuck Jr. flew that night from Alaska to Richland to be at his side. When they arrived, Clem was already in a coma. They held his hand and talked to him as he lingered near death. As he was about to slip away, his longtime friend and priest, Father O'Shea, administered the last rites. By then, Clem had been in a coma for three days, but when the priest started reciting the Lord's Prayer,

Clem sat up and prayed it with him. At the conclusion, he smiled, took Father O'Shea's hand, and said, "Thanks, Bishop." Then he caught himself. "Hey wait!" he exclaimed. "You're not a bishop. You're a priest!" He then lay back on his pillow and within a few hours he was dead.

I found it no mere coincidence that 1992, the year of Clem's death, also marked the year Sarah entered politics in the race for a seat on the Wasilla City Council. Members of our family who knew both Clem and Sarah saw striking similarities between them. He eschewed campaign donations and sought to win a seat on the Richland City Council without a high-dollar campaign. All of Sarah's campaigns were marked by the same grassroots effort, including hand-painted signs during her run for city council and mayor. She was willing to work day and night to accomplish her goals, but asking someone for a donation went against the grain for her. It ran counter to all that she learned from us and from life in our family. We taught our children to overcome obstacles by working harder. The notion of asking someone to give her something she hadn't earned was more than just a foreign idea. It was contrary to her internal ethos. Lack of money wasn't much of an impediment in local elections, but as she moved into statewide elections it made campaigning a little more difficult.

Some who knew Sarah were surprised when she entered the city council race. They'd seen her as an athlete and as a sports reporter, but they'd never pictured her as a candidate for office. "She was always such a shy and sweet girl," her coach Reid Smith remembered. "I was totally surprised when she entered politics." Others were caught off guard as well, but once she announced her intention to seek office, they had little doubt she would succeed. In the words of Reid, most found her to be "a politician I can relate to."

In 2002, Sarah entered the Republican primary as a candidate for lieutenant governor. The field was crowded with five candidates. Sally and I were away in Palmyra, an atoll in the Pacific Ocean south of Hawaii. We were there for most of the campaign on a previously arranged work assignment with the USDA. I didn't like the idea of Sarah entering the race, primarily because I knew she would be facing some powerful people who were backed by lots of money. I also knew Sarah's distaste for asking for money would hamper her ability to be effective. None of us realized she was developing a new approach to campaigning, one that relied more on volunteers and less on hiring others to do the work.

Sarah was also hampered in that lieutenant governor's race by her message. She campaigned on a pro-Alaska, fiscally conservative message and called for "new energy" in state government. That message articulated a vision that was more suited to a bid for governor. In Alaska, the lieutenant governor's position is a working job, but it doesn't provide a platform for reform. Still, she campaigned hard, developed a statewide organization of volunteers, and closed to within a few points of the leader shortly before the election. But it wasn't enough and she came in second to Loren Leman, the eventual winner in the general election.

Losing was never easy for Sarah. Whether it was basketball in high school or politics in a statewide election, she played to win. Accepting any finishing position other than first place ran counter to her competitive nature, and she would never agree that coming in second was a good thing—except perhaps in this case.

After Frank Murkowski won the governor's race that year, he appointed Sarah to the Oil and Gas Conservation Commission. Very quickly, she was named the commission's chairperson. What she saw from that position inside the administration helped her realize the blessing she'd received in not winning the lieutenant governor's race. It also showed her that her instincts about how to run a campaign were right. She could be effective at a statewide level without selling her soul to the powerful interests who traditionally controlled Alaska politics.

As 2006 drew near, and with it a new election cycle, rumors spread that Sarah was considering a second bid for lieutenant governor. Friends and supporters from the previous campaign, like Don and Sharon Benson and Kerm Ketchum, started calling her and encouraging her to avoid the lieutenant governor's race and run for governor instead. Don remembered, "When I heard she was thinking about lieutenant governor again, I picked up the phone and called her. And I kept calling her. 'Don't do that. Run for governor.'"

Others contacted her as well and through the summer of 2005 she continued to deliberate. Though she consulted Todd and bounced her ideas off others with political experience, the process of deciding whether to enter the race seemed primarily a debate within her own mind. Could she be effective, could she make a difference, could she win, could she energize the call for change regardless of whether she won or lost?

Finally, in October 2005, before a packed living room at her home, Sarah announced her decision. She was running for governor. I was concerned for what that meant to her personally—the strain it would put on her life—and, to be frank, I thought she was in over her head politically. I had no doubt she could do the job as governor, but getting there was another matter. As with the lieutenant governor's campaign four years earlier, she faced some very powerful, well-funded, seasoned politicians, all of whom had done this before and knew how to play the political game at its darkest, most cutthroat level. I was worried about how things would turn out for her.

Sarah's announcement came early, which gave her an advantage. She also had a volunteer network already in place from the lieutenant governor's campaign. They hadn't been formally organized during the interim but they were there just the same. They went to work immediately. "We put up signs all over the Mat-Su Valley," Don recalled. "Tara Jollie worked in the office and sent us lists of people who wanted yard signs. In the evening after work we went out in the truck, tracked down the locations, and put up the signs."

They also began an Internet group that operated on its own, apart from the campaign. Members of that group manned their computers and searched for blogs and news sites with articles about the governor's race. Using multiple e-mail accounts, and sometimes multiple computers, they made it their own personal mission to post responses to every news article that touched on the issues and candidates. They diligently and relentlessly countered every negative comment and encouraged every positive response, not just with partisan invective but with well-researched facts.

At the same time, Sarah pushed herself to become a better fund-raiser. "We started out doing events and maybe four people would show up," Don remembered. Undeterred, Sarah focused on connecting with the people who showed up. "Sarah's a people person," Don continued. "When she talks to you she makes you feel like you are the only person in the world." Her focus on engaging potential supporters helped get them personally involved with the campaign. Gradually, attendance at the events improved and went from just a few at the beginning to hundreds before the campaign ended.

That approach didn't yield many large contributions—most of her financial support during the primary came from small, individual donations—but it gave her an ever-expanding network of volunteers. What she lacked in money, those volunteers made up for with personal involvement. "People were tired of Murkowski," Lew Bradley recalled. "They wanted a change." And they wanted it enough to get out and work for it. In the words of our friend O. P. Ditch, "She was someone who's in it for the right reasons," and those right reasons attracted a large cadre of willing supporters. Sarah wasn't willing to sell out those goals and ideals for "politics as usual" at the hand of large donors.

Bruce Anders, a lawyer with the Attorney General's Office during the 2006 gubernatorial election, was drawn to Sarah's campaign by her fresh ideas and innovative approach. He worked as a volunteer writing position papers and helping with Sarah's speeches. "We worked out of a cramped headquarters and were totally outspent by the other candidates in the primary." He remembered oil-company representatives stopping by the office. "They were ushered into Sarah's office for a meeting. Many of them came with a donation check in hand. All they wanted in exchange was favorable consideration on some of the issues." Sarah would have none of it. "She said, 'There's the door,' and they were shown the way out."

Those were tough decisions. The campaign really could have used the money. But in a world where values are often little more than a slogan, especially from political candidates, Sarah knew that integrity was everything. She couldn't campaign against corruption while taking the same contributions she said were at the heart of the state's problems. If she was going to campaign against corruption, she had to do it in a manner that was above reproach. To do that, to run a successful campaign without accepting large contributions from traditional political players, she needed volunteers who would make up the difference with work. As the campaign developed, volunteers showed up in droves.

Jeff Wheaton, a teacher working two jobs to make ends meet, joined us on a busy street corner in Anchorage to wave our Sarah Palin signs and shout at passing motorists. He was friends with Chuck Jr. and had come to know Heather, Sarah, and Molly through him. When Jeff learned that Sarah was running for governor, he wanted to help but he didn't have much time. He gave an hour each morning and afternoon to stand on that street corner with us. "The thing I noticed was the passion," Jeff remembered. "There were just the four of us at first, but we were enthusiastic and the people who passed and honked their horns at us seemed enthusiastic. Before long, our small group expanded and we had a crowd out there."

Don Benson, and the Internet organization that developed around Anchorage, was very helpful, but he and his group weren't unique among those working for Sarah. Similar volunteers and groups emerged in Fairbanks and Juneau, the state's other major urban areas. In Anchorage, businessmen like Dave Eibeck helped by placing signs at their businesses and in the yards of their homes. "I was attracted by her policy and ideals," Dave remembered. "And by the fact that she was an evangelical. That was important to me."

People who lived in the bush got involved too. Frank Gurtler, who lived way out in Manley Hot Springs, Alaska, had a yard sign at his house and was a vocal Sarah supporter. Many others in the bush did the same. As she already knew, those volunteers turned out to be as good as gold. Some of them stood on the street corner in sub-freezing weather, waving campaign signs and shouting at passing motorists. Others worked long hours in the campaign office, fielding phone calls, answering mail, and responding to e-mail messages. Everyone worked for free and they were glad to be there. Sarah had a close circle of personal friends, too, many of whom she met in an aerobics class. They provided emotional support, looked after the children, and kept her grounded in "real life" apart from the hectic campaign.

Phil Schneider, one of Chuck Jr.'s friends, had taken a year away from his job as a school principal in order to travel with his wife. As the campaign picked up speed, he used much of that time to volunteer with the campaign. Initially attracted to Sarah through his friendship with Chuck, he quickly found her to be "honest and forthright." Not long after he joined the campaign, he took over scheduling and helped organize it into a system that kept Sarah in the right place at the right time with the necessary preparation to be successful.

Clark and Kris Perry attended the October meeting when Sarah made her announcement. They volunteered right from the beginning. Kris was president of the Chamber of Commerce when Sarah was mayor. They had become good friends through their common experiences in dealing with city issues and in rearing their children. She and Clark were longtime supporters of Sarah's political career, even before she entered the gubernatorial race. Clark's job afforded him extra time to devote to the campaign and he became involved immediately. His efforts included unique fund-raising ideas that proved very helpful, especially in the early stages of the race. Kris initially had less time available, but after Sarah won the primary she took a leave of absence from her job to manage the general election effort.

Sally, Chuck Jr., Heather, and Molly worked tirelessly too. Everyone pitched in, even a few of her opponents' volunteers. I remember standing with Don Benson, Adrian Lane, and Brian Timblin on a corner in Wasilla, braving the cold in the months before the election, waving campaign signs and harassing passing motorists. A guy showed up from one of the other candidates with a sign questioning Sarah's qualifications. Rather than throwing him in the ditch, we engaged him with the friendly banter we used in conversation among ourselves and gently challenged him to tell us the reason he opposed Sarah. After spending time with us, he threw his anti-Sarah sign in the ditch, picked up one of her signs, and joined us as we waved and shouted at passing motorists.

On Election Day, we all gathered on street corners in Anchorage and near our homes to wave signs and shout at passing motorists one last time. I don't know how much influence it had on voters but maybe we reminded a few of them to vote. Sarah joined us for a while, then drifted over to the Captain Cook Hotel, where preparations were under way for an election-night watch and victory celebration. Mary Havens, a volunteer who later worked in the governor's office, remembered, "Sarah was there with us, helping set up tables for the party. That's just the way she was." That's the way the campaign had been too. Everyone doing what needed to be done, without regard for titles or positions.

People across the state responded in a similar manner, gathering on street corners to cheer and wave their signs, going door-to-door to hand out leaflets, making phone calls, and generating pro-Sarah e-mails. For the most part, however, it was Sarah who made the real difference, a point emphasized by Bruce Anders at the inauguration. When I thanked him for helping Sarah win, he politely demurred and suggested his help had not been all that significant. And then, with a gesture to the room where we were standing and in which Sarah had just taken the oath of office, he added, "The truth is—Sarah is here because Sarah wanted to be here."

After Sarah became governor, Don Benson and the Internet group that had worked hard during the campaign suddenly had nothing to do and "went underground," as Don describes it. A few were offered positions in Sarah's administration but most resumed the daily lives they'd lived before the campaign and returned to their typical pre-campaign routine. That lasted about three months.

On February 2, 2007, Adam Brickley, a student at the University of Colorado, created a blog entitled *Draft Sarah Palin for Vice President*. His first entry offered an argument for why she should be named as the vice presidential running mate for Rudy Giuliani, at the time the front runner for the Republican nomination for president in the 2008 election. Don and the pro-Sarah Internet group learned about the blog a few days later and immediately began organizing support for a push to get Sarah on the ticket.

As they had done during the gubernatorial campaign, they searched the Internet for related blogs and news sites, where they posted comments and directed users to Brickley's blog. They located websites that invited users to vote in vice presidential preferential polls and made sure they voted for Sarah. With polls that did not include her name, they posted comments suggesting her as an alternative to others then being considered and encouraged sites to add her name to the list. Their help moved Sarah's name up in several of the informal polls, not all the way to the top but high enough to get her noticed. That, in turn, generated discussion about her among news outlets. Before long she wasn't just the first female governor of Alaska. She was on the short list of names mentioned as a potential Republican vice presidential candidate.

I'm pro-life. I'll do all I can to see every baby is created with a future and potential. The legislature should do all it can to protect human life.

Sarah Palin

CHAPTER 15

True North Never Changes

Values are what you do when no one's looking. People today
want to know if their leaders can live it when the cameras
are off and no one is watching.
CHUCK HEATH JR.

With the rise of conservative Christian political involvement in the 1970s, "values" became the watchword of politics. Emphasis on that topic has influenced elections for more than two decades. More than ever, people want to know if their leaders can live the life they suggest for everyone else. Voters aren't nearly so interested in whether a politician gives mental assent to an ideal as they are in whether that ideal has any bearing on the here-and-now of the politician's life. Can you live it when the ideal falls at a tough place in your own life? Someone once said, "Values are what you do when no one's looking." People today want to know if their leaders can live the life they espouse when the cameras are off and no one is watching.

One of the hallmarks of our present era is the never-ending quest for authenticity—to live a life of meaning. When we were younger, no one used the term "authentic." Instead, they talked about living with "consistency." Our parents were classic examples. Dad might have been crusty and abrupt, and his word was

175

always the law, but he was always the same. Things that were wrong today were wrong tomorrow, and what he expected of us he also expected of himself. He encouraged us to take up the sport of distance running, and he ran himself. He expected us to maintain grades at the top of our class, and he was a lifelong learner too. We were expected to own up to our mistakes and face the consequences. He did the same with his own errors.

Whatever we did, he demanded we do to the best of our ability, and he demanded the same from himself. We all had to work, and he worked too—often working two or three jobs at once. He didn't attend church much, but if we signed up for a program with the youth group he made sure we followed through and gave it our best. Always a coach, he often reduced his principles to simple, pithy statements. "Don't toot your own horn. If you're any good, someone else will toot it for you." The one I liked was, "When you get to the end zone, act like you've been there before." Mari Rich, principal at Chugiak Elementary School when he taught there, said, "He was honest, sensitive, stern—but fair—and he was consistent. He wasn't wishy-washy."

Mom, on the other hand, was nurturing, caring, and very much a mother. She disciplined us when we got out of hand, but that usually wasn't necessary. Most of the time, she was able to convince us to behave by providing a great example for us to follow. Often, she maneuvered us into doing what needed to be done, and did it in a way that made us think it was our idea all along. People sometimes tell me that Sarah got the best of both our parents. If she got her sense of adventure from Dad, she got her humility from Mom.

While Sarah was still mayor, my friend Jeff Wheaton got to know my sisters Heather and Molly. He met Heather through church. I'm not exactly sure how he came to know Molly. I met him when we worked together at the same elementary school. Jeff is a long-distance runner, and one day he mentioned to Heather that he was entered in a race in Wasilla. Heather reminded him that Sarah lived there and suggested the two might meet. She told him, "Sarah looks sort of like me, only she has dark hair." That Saturday, after checking in for the race, Jeff wandered around looking for Sarah. He found a woman sitting alone at a table cutting oranges into bite-size slices. Jeff wasn't sure who she was, but he approached the table. "Are you Sarah?"

Sarah turned to him with a smile. "You must be Jeff. Heather said you were coming for the race." And with that the two struck up a friendship—the mayor of Wasilla with orange juice on her hands, working as an unnoticed volunteer at a long-distance race. She got that humble character from our mother.

Christy Ridenour, a nuclear medical technician from Indianapolis, noticed that trait in Sarah too. She met Sarah on the campaign trail, visited with her at several book signings, and became a friend of the family. Commenting on Sarah, she said, "There aren't many people who have risen as high as she has in politics who, when you meet them, are who they say they are. With Sarah, what you see is what you get."

Mom and Dad taught us good, old-fashioned American values. Work hard, stick to your job, see a project through, have respect for yourself and others. Mom made sure we did our best to meet those expectations. She also made sure we had an opportunity to know the Lord and understand what He expected of us. Most of the time, the two were the same.

Our parents taught by example. They lived what they believed and taught us to do likewise. As adults, we have all faced our own challenges but we faced them with values that guided us through difficult circumstances. The difference for Heather, Molly, and me is that we had the luxury of facing most of those challenges in relative privacy, away from the public eye. Sarah, by reason of the political life she chose, was forced to face her personal challenges in public. As the events of 2008 unfolded, she confronted circumstances that challenged two of her deepest convictions—the value of human life, and the need for a strong national defense. By coincidence, both involved her sons.

From the time Sarah first entered politics as a candidate for a seat on the Wasilla City Council, she has voiced a strong pro-life position. For her and for us, life is sacred and it begins at conception. She believed that then, when she was young and the prospect of a full career lay before her, and she believed it in December 2007 when, at the age of forty-three, she learned she was pregnant with a child who had Down syndrome.

Down syndrome is a chromosomal condition. It is caused by the presence of an extra twenty-first chromosome or portion thereof. The condition can cause physical and cognitive impairment. Children who are born with Down syndrome often face difficult challenges. They also bring a tremendous blessing to supportive and caring families. Medical science has come a long way in diagnosing the condition. Tests are available to determine a family's propensity for carrying the syndrome. After a woman becomes pregnant, amniocentesis can determine if the fetus has the condition. Ninety percent of the women who learn they are carrying a child with Down syndrome abort the pregnancy. That was never an option for Sarah.

I didn't learn Sarah was pregnant with Trig until she and Todd announced the news to the world, about six months into the pregnancy. Many people don't believe that, but it's true. Mom and Dad learned the news the same way. She didn't tell her friends, either, though many of them who saw her on a regular basis suspected it from changes in her physical appearance. That she didn't tell us beforehand was not a big issue. Sarah has always been a private person. In the words of longtime friend Carol Ryan, "That girl can keep a secret." She wasn't particularly forthcoming about news of her previous pregnancies and I'm sure that knowing she was carrying a child with Down syndrome made her even more reluctant to talk.

Having learned of the pregnancy with the public announcement, I was not privy to Sarah's thoughts or her state of mind when she learned of Trig's condition. But I know my sister well enough to know that she never once considered anything but giving birth to him. She might have wrestled with how she personally would handle the demands of raising him and caring for him. She might have wondered if she was capable. But she would have wondered those things while she was facing into the wind and staring the future in the eye. Todd was of the same opinion. When posed with the question of "Why did this happen to us?" his response was, "Why *not* us?"

In the years since Trig's birth, the wisdom of Todd and Sarah's choice has been all the more evident. "Trig," in the words of a close family friend, "*made* that family. He is the sunshine of her [Sarah's] life and the lives of a lot of people." Todd and Sarah are both achievers and have led an active, goal-oriented life, much of it focused on physical, athletic competition. Both of them are very competitive and they raised their children to be the same, always challenging them to push themselves to do more. Trig upset that lifestyle, in a good way. Caring for him took them beyond themselves.

Trig's birth came early in 2008. His arrival was met with celebration and the sober acknowledgment that his presence in our lives would change us all. We didn't realize how much he would teach us about ourselves, about caring for one another, and about our commitment to one another as a family. But that's not all that year had in store for us. That same year, Sarah's eldest son, Track, was deployed to Iraq with his Army unit. A lot has changed in that country since then, but when he was sent there it was still a hostile combat zone.

While we were not a political family, we were patriotic. Both of our grandfathers participated in the effort to defend the nation during World War II—Charlie as a Navy photographer and Clem as an employee at Hanford. On our mother's side of the family, many of our aunts and uncles served in the US Air Force. Dad served in the Army during the 1950s, and was a lifelong World War II history buff. One of the few times he would actually sit with us to watch television was when a movie about World War II was playing. He had a profound sense of gratitude for those who risked their lives to defend our country, and he passed that on to us.

During Sarah's senior year in high school, Ronald Reagan was elected president. He quickly became one of Sarah's heroes and her favorite president. She was inspired by his no-nonsense approach to government and by his unabashed American pride. As she entered into political life she sought to emulate his approach and fashioned her own version of what used to be called "compassionate conservatism"—the notion that free enterprise was the key to solving many of our problems, but that prosperity brings with it an obligation to care for the poor. She and Reagan might have differed on the details of that position, but when it came to national defense they would have been in complete agreement. Sarah is a genuine advocate for maintaining a strong national defense.

During the 2008 campaign, some derided her for suggesting the proximity of the Alaskan coast to the coast of Russia made her uniquely aware of the need for a strong military. More than one commentator pointed out that Russia was no longer our nemesis, as it had been during the Cold War. Whether Russia is our primary adversary or not remains to be seen. However, having grown up here in the 1960s and 1970s, we were well aware that the Soviet military was not merely a theoretical enemy of America's heartland. It was an enemy close at hand with weapons pointed in our direction. Sarah understood that. So did the Pentagon. That's why Alaska, though forty-seventh in size by state population, has six military bases, three Coast Guard installations, and hosts a number of early-warning radar sites.

Sarah's pro-military stance became more real to all of us on September 11, 2007, when her eldest son, Track, marked the September 11 anniversary by enlisting in the US Army. I don't recall talking to him about the decision. Dad, who had enlisted right out of high school, knew Army life wasn't as glamorous as recruiters and movies describe and tried to discuss it with him on several occasions. Track never gave a clear answer for his motivation, other than a desire to serve his country. He was young, a little undisciplined—though not a problem—and fully imbued with the sense of invulnerability only youth can bring. After high school, he played junior hockey in a developmental league and did well. He liked the physical nature of the game and the challenge of competition. If he had kept at it, he could have enjoyed a career as a professional. College was an option too, but he chose the Army instead.

Track went through basic training at Fort Benning, Georgia. When he finished, he invited Todd and Sarah to attend his graduation. Sarah was scheduled to address the Alaska legislature the day before with her annual State of the State speech and asked to move the time an hour earlier to allow her to make the trip to

Georgia. At the last minute, Lyda Green, president of the state senate and elected from our district, decided the time wouldn't work. Her intransigence on the issue quickly became a lead story in the state news outlets and occupied the attention of several radio talk-show hosts. Sarah thought it was a tempest in a teapot, except for the statements made by some who seemed to think military service was "no big deal." Defending our nation has always been a very big deal with Sarah.

Eventually, Sarah and Lyda Green worked out their differences. Sarah gave the speech and made it to Georgia in time to see Track graduate, but adjusting her schedule meant missing many of the preliminary events on base. The controversy also further soured Sarah's relationship with Lyda.

After basic training, Track was assigned to the first brigade of the Twenty-Fifth Infantry Division, a Stryker unit with the nickname "Arctic Thunder." Stryker teams operate an eight-wheeled armored vehicle that carries a crew of eleven infantry. It is especially effective in urban warfare. In Iraq, Stryker units saw heavy action and were critical in gaining control of the major cities. Track and his unit deployed to Iraq in 2008, not long after the Republican National Convention. While we were immersed in a political campaign, he was immersed in a military one.

We all knew he was entering a dangerous combat zone and that members of Stryker units were often the target of enemy attacks. The vehicles had been specially designed to counter the threat of improvised explosive devices used by terrorists and insurgents in tactics that had proved effective and lethal during the first days of the war. Just how dangerous that situation was came home to me not long after Track left the country.

As part of my work in education, I traveled to Fort Richardson, an Army installation on the outskirts of Anchorage. It has since merged with Elmendorf Air Force Base, but back then it was still a separate facility. I went there to observe teachers using reading curricula at Ursa Minor Elementary School. As I talked to a class of eight-year-olds, I learned that all but three students came from homes where one or both parents were deployed to either Iraq or Afghanistan. Those children—practically the entire class—faced the very real possibility that one or both of their parents would not return alive. That's when the reality of Track's situation hit me.

Sarah didn't back away from support of a strong national defense, even when defending the country meant watching her own son as he was deployed to a combat zone. She was proud he enlisted to defend our country and was willing to bear her own burden of worry, just as thousands of other mothers have done in the past and are doing today. When she spoke about the need for a strong military, she knew the gravity of that stance. She knew that she was asking other parents to send their sons and daughters into potentially deadly situations. Yet she wasn't asking them to do anything more than she had already done herself.

She brought the same sense of passion and commitment to other issues as well. The basin around Cook Inlet contains almost one-half of the known US coal reserves. It is also home to rich deposits of oil and natural gas. Above those mineral deposits lies some of the most gorgeous landscape on earth, teeming with wildlife. When we talk about resource development, we aren't talking about drilling or mining in someone else's backyard. We're talking about developing the resources that rest beneath our feet and within our grasp, literally. Most of Alaska is equally as beautiful and equally as rich in resources as our area.

We grew up hunting the woods of Alaska and fishing its bays and streams. Our parents instilled in us a love of nature. Every time we entered the woods on a hunting or camping trip, Dad repeated one of his favorite mantras, "Leave it better than you found it." When we camped, we did our best to contain our trash within the confines of our own campsite and when we left, we hauled out whatever we brought in. Sometimes, we carried away the trash others left behind too.

Sarah has been quoted often on the issue of drilling for oil. "Drill, baby, drill," and "Drill here, drill now," became slogans for her and her followers. Living in Alaska, we've seen firsthand that oil production doesn't have to mean the end of a clean, safe environment. The extraction of energy, whether it's coal, oil, gas, or even nuclear, is a dangerous business. It does have an effect on the environment, but so do many other things we find desirable, and although most human activity changes the ecosystem, those consequences don't have to be negative.

Sarah's view of resource development goes beyond simply drilling for oil or mining other minerals and includes the active management of the state's wildlife. She has been attacked by the media for her position on that subject, but almost no one has bothered to understand the issue. For centuries native Alaskans lived off the land. They hunted, fished, and trapped animals in the wild to gather the food they needed. Almost nothing went to waste. They ate the flesh, used the hides to make clothing, and rendered the fat into oil, which they used for cooking and as fuel. In those days, the human population was small in relation to the game. Harvesting wildlife had little effect on the balance of the animal population. The ecosystem readily accommodated the activity.

Today, the human population has risen. Even in Alaska, as large as it is, human conduct affects wildlife in ways that the natural ecosystem can't address. Encroachment on habitat and modern hunting practices often throw the predator/prey ratio out of balance, making it necessary for wildlife experts to intervene. That's what happened in the famous spat over the use of helicopters in shooting wolves. Reporters portrayed the practice as bloodthirsty hunters taking unfair advantage of hapless wild creatures. That was simply untrue. The practice was controlled by state biologists and wildlife officials in an attempt to reduce the wolf population in order to allow the moose and caribou populations to rise to normal levels.

Lew Bradley, a Fish and Wildlife board member during Sarah's administration, explained it this way. "We weren't talking about 'fair practices.' Our policy was aimed at the surgical removal of excess wolf population." In fact, helicopters seldom were used for that purpose—by some accounts only twice—and then only because the wolves roamed through inaccessible terrain. They are wily creatures, and by the time hunters could get to their location on foot, they often were gone.

The policy of monitoring and adjusting the wildlife population was consistent with the state constitution's mandate that government manage the state's natural resources "for abundance" and was supported by former governor Frank Murkowski and current governor Sean Parnell. It was also supported by native Alaskans who lived in the interior portion of the state and relied on the availability of moose and caribou as a source of protein in their diet.

Not all of our family members are hunters, but we do all agree on one thing. The right of individuals to "keep and bear arms," a right preserved in the Second Amendment to the federal Constitution, is an essential right for every American. It's important to us and to the nation. I understand that we approach this issue from the perspective of hunters who enjoy the outdoors and live in a rural state where most of the land is wild and unsettled. People who live in densely populated urban areas view things differently. I understand that. They're more interested in preventing crime and curtailing the mayhem firearms can produce when wielded by thugs and criminals. However, taking away all firearms from everyone is not the solution to that issue. People who grow up with guns and are taught to use them properly are much less apt to use them irresponsibly.

During World War II, after attacking the Navy fleet at Pearl Harbor, the Japanese had a clear shot at the California coast. I've often wondered why they didn't invade, especially in light of information about their later attempts to bomb the coast. They actually occupied the Aleutian Islands but didn't attempt to land anywhere else along the coast. A recent Internet article suggested one important reason was that the Japanese realized millions of US citizens were armed and knew how to handle their weapons. I don't know if that story is correct, but the United States is home to more than ten million deer hunters. That would give us the largest army in the world. Many scoff at the notion of an armed citizenry resisting the will of tyrants, often pointing out that a hunting rifle is no match for modern weapons of war and sophisticated combat systems. That may be true, but that's also the same thing the British said about the American colonists before the American Revolution.

Sarah's friend Melanie Messenger summed up Sarah's views when she said, "Sarah believes that the people who wrote the Constitution knew what they were doing and we need to get back to those checks and balances."

Many needlessly hurtful things have been said and written about Sarah, challenging her faith, integrity, values, and character. Jeannie DeAngelis, a writer for *American Thinker*, recently suggested the problem with those comments isn't with Sarah but with the nation. We've become a nation that gives lip service to values. When someone arrives on the scene who actually tries to live from the values she espouses, who attempts to allow those values to inform her life—religiously, politically, personally—that person, by her mere presence, challenges our shortcomings in those areas. The light of truth, however dimly or brightly it may shine from Sarah's life, casts a revealing glare across the darkness that pervades American popular culture. Many would rather close their eyes to that light than endure the pain of the self-examination it demands.

I fought to bring about the largest private-sector infrastructure project in North American history. And when that deal was struck, we began a nearly forty-billion-dollar natural gas pipeline to help lead America to energy independence.

Sarah Palin

CHAPTER 16

Being Governor

*Hard work and long hours didn't just apply to staff
and administration officials. Sarah imposed the
same regimen on herself, too.*
CHUCK HEATH SR.

W
ith the exception of two states, New Hampshire and
Vermont, the governors of every state in the Union
serve four-year terms. At first glance, that sounds like a lot of time.
Political reality, however, reduces that time to a much shorter
period.

For the typical governor entering a first term, the initial six
months in office are usually spent assembling an administration and learning the rudiments of the job. Not long after that,
the election cycle begins for members of the state legislature. In
Alaska, the entire House of Representatives and one-half of the
Senate stand for reelection every two years. Not much gets done
during the months surrounding those elections. Shortly after the
new legislature takes office, the governor's own reelection effort
begins. That leaves the governor with only two years of effective
governing time—730 days. Sarah was well aware of the limitations imposed on both her time and her effectiveness.

During the campaign, she laid out several key areas she

proposed to address, most notably ethics reform, resource development, education, and infrastructure. However, to be effective, she had to translate those lofty ideas into concrete policies and actions. She could have turned to organizational charts, well-drawn plans, and neatly crafted strategies, which would have produced a "politics as usual" solution. Instead, she approached it like a coach and looked for people who could lead by example. Then she empowered them to accomplish their goals and turned them loose to do their job.

In the brief transition between election and inauguration—she was elected in November and sworn into office in December—Sarah sought qualified people who could be ready to make things happen the minute they took office. Bruce Anders worked with Sarah on the proposed new gas pipeline issue during the campaign and became part of the gasline team when her administration turned to the task of preparing legislation to get the pipeline built. Many of Bruce's campaign position papers on the issue provided the fundamental structure of the gasline legislation that was at the forefront of Sarah's term in office. He saw firsthand how she assembled her team and tackled the issues. "She wanted as many perspectives as possible," Bruce remembered. "The best people, the smartest people with the best ideas, even from the Murkowski folks."

One of the people Sarah chose for a key position was Meghan Stapleton. At the time Sarah was elected, Meghan was working as a spokesperson for Alaska Communications Systems, an integrated telecommunications company. Before that, she had enjoyed a successful career as a television reporter and news anchor. She was also a supporter of one of Sarah's opponents in the primary campaign, but Sarah had seen Meghan's work, knew her reputation, and wanted her help. "After the election, when [Sarah] asked to meet with me, I told my husband I wasn't interested in a job but since it was the governor asking, I had to at least take the meeting." That meeting changed her mind. "I was totally blown away. She was not the same person I saw in the campaign. She was bright, incredibly intelligent, articulate, charming. I remember thinking, 'If Alaskans had only seen this, the election would have never been in question.'" Sarah offered Meghan the combined position of director of communications and press secretary, a position she readily accepted.

Meghan took the job thinking she had an opportunity to make a difference for Alaska. She knew a position like that would involve long hours and lots of work but even knowing that, she was surprised by the level of interest Sarah's election generated. "I couldn't believe the star power she brought. When she walked into the room and started talking to you, it was like that was the only conversation in the room. She had this magnetic personality that generated all kinds of attention." Meghan and her fledgling staff faced a challenge. "We had requests for interviews coming from not just Alaska but across the country." Keeping up with those requests took hours of long, hard work.

After Sarah was elected governor, she appointed a committee that planned the inauguration ceremony. The fiftieth anniversary of Alaska's admittance to statehood was approaching and Sarah wanted to hold the inauguration in Fairbanks, where the state constitution had been drafted. The committee chartered five buses to transport family, friends, and supporters to the event. A number of people from Wasilla were included in the traveling group, but not everyone who knew us received an invitation.

Sally and I rode one of the buses to Fairbanks and participated in a number of events leading up to the ceremony when Sarah took the oath of office. On Inauguration Day, we joined her in

Founders Hall and sat behind her on the dais as she placed her hand on the Bible and swore to uphold the state constitution and diligently execute her duties as governor. Then we watched as she gave her first speech as the state's highest executive officer. As a father, it was quite an experience seeing our daughter ascend to the most powerful office in the state. I always knew Sarah would go far in life—as I expected of all our children—but I never thought of her as an elected official. Not as a member of the city council or as mayor, and certainly not as governor. To say I was proud would be an understatement.

From our vantage point seated behind her while she spoke, I looked across the room and saw in the audience many of her friends and supporters of every kind. People we'd known since coming to Alaska, some we'd met for the first time during the campaign, and a few we'd known from our life in Idaho. Most had worked day and night to get Sarah elected. Some had actively promoted her candidacy even before she officially entered the campaign. I was proud of their work and even prouder to know that they had volunteered, most of them without being asked. They devoted their time, energy, and resources to our daughter's campaign and helped her accomplish a goal many thought unattainable.

Also seated in the crowd that day were people who'd worked just as hard for Murkowski and Knowles. They were staunch opponents who'd fought serious, well-financed efforts to keep Sarah from winning, first in the primary and then in the general election. Many of them held an honest difference of opinion on the underlying issues and approached government from a fundamentally different perspective. Others worked from a more sinister motive. Yet they were all smiles that day and in spite of the comments many had made during the campaign, they had only good things to say about Sarah. I was disgusted by the way they tried to ingratiate themselves after they were defeated.

In the days following the inauguration, Sarah worked hard to assemble an administration staffed with people who were committed to the task of attaining the goals she'd outlined during the campaign. Many of those same people I saw at the inauguration—people who had fought hard to defeat Sarah and who had attacked her during the campaign—lined up to give her their résumés and ask for an administrative appointment. I would have shown them the door and let them know in no uncertain terms what I thought of them, but not Sarah. She just smiled and nodded and graciously entertained their requests. She even appointed some of them to government positions.

Most of the people in Wasilla shared our enthusiasm for Sarah's success and were genuinely glad that a person from our town was elected governor of the state. Not all of them voted for Sarah and even her supporters didn't agree with her on every issue, but the people who lived in our area—Wasilla, Palmer, Willow, the Mat-Su Valley—were generally supportive. Most, but not everyone.

One person who wasn't invited along for the bus ride to the inauguration was a woman we'd known for thirty years. I taught her children in school and we'd always considered her a friend. She was a longtime Democrat and a vocal supporter of Tony Knowles, the man Sarah had just defeated in the gubernatorial election. That she supported Sarah's opponent didn't change the way I thought about her. I never based my friendship with anyone solely on their political perspective. Apparently she didn't see things that way.

Not long after the inauguration, I was standing in line at the post office and she was there. When she saw me, she moved closer and—without provocation from me or anyone else—roared at me in a loud voice, "Just because your daughter is governor, you think you can do anything you want to in this town. I and my family want nothing to do with you or your family now!"

Later, when Sarah became the 2008 Republican nominee for vice president, someone from a national magazine tracked the woman down and interviewed her. She unloaded on them with her opinion about Sarah and the rest of us. The magazine used that interview as the basis for a scathing article about Sarah. Not long after it appeared in print, three of the woman's children called us to apologize for their mother's behavior.

Shortly after Sarah was sworn in as governor, we flew down to Juneau to attend a dinner at the governor's mansion. Sally and I enjoyed seeing the antiques that had accumulated there over the years and the cases filled with gifts from dignitaries who visited the state. Later that day, after the official festivities were over, Chuck Jr. and I went down to the basement to watch a football game on television. While we were watching, one of the house-maids came down and asked if we wanted a snack. We both said, "Sure," and she asked us what we wanted. Chuck Jr. jokingly said, "Oh, I don't know. How about some king crab." Twenty minutes later a huge platter arrived, piled high with crab legs. We were shocked that they actually served it to us, but not too shocked to accept.

Not long after our visit, Sarah put a stop to that kind of extravagance. She thought it was hypocritical to tell Alaskans they needed to be fiscally conservative while she and her family lived the high life in the mansion. So, she dismissed the chef and the maid and told us we were all fully capable of cooking our own meals and cleaning up after ourselves. She took the same approach with her car.

Previous governors traveled with a driver and bodyguard. Sarah didn't want that. On most days, she drove herself to wherever she needed to go. She actually enjoyed the time alone in the car while driving to and from appointments. She said it was one of the few times during the day when she could think in solitude. The agents assigned to protect her didn't like it, but she insisted on traveling that way. After the 2008 campaign with John McCain she was forced to endure tighter security, but until then she insisted she was fine on her own.

While she was changing things in Juneau, Sarah sold the state jet, too. Her predecessor, Frank Murkowski, had purchased the airplane supposedly on the notion that it traveled faster than the prop planes the state already owned and would make travel more efficient. The legislature objected to the idea but he bought the plane anyway. It was fast all right, but most of the rural airstrips in Alaska are paved with gravel, making it impossible for the jet to land on them. That jet became a symbol of how out of touch Murkowski was with life in Alaska. In her first week as governor, Sarah had it listed for sale on eBay. Although the plane eventually sold at a loss, her decision to get rid of it saved the state hundreds of thousands of dollars in annual operating and maintenance expenses.

After her first few months in office, Sarah and Todd decided to avoid life in the Juneau governor's mansion and instead remain in Wasilla. They had young children in school with established routines, friends, and activities. Moving to Juneau merely to maintain an official residence in the mansion seemed to Sarah like a waste of time and money. Except when the legislature was in session, she worked from the governor's office in Anchorage. The Anchorage offices were really the heart of state government anyway and were within driving distance of most Alaskans. Juneau, by contrast, was completely cut off from the state highway system and accessible only by air and water.

Not everyone was comfortable with the changes Sarah made or her attempts at conducting state business in an open, transparent, and inclusive manner. Some officials retained from the Murkowski administration were not as interested as Sarah was in rising above partisan politics, either. In addition, the state Republican Party establishment remained staunchly opposed to her, in spite of her overwhelming victory in the election.

Many permanent state government employees were opposed to her too, and saw her new, fresh approach to old government problems as a threat to their entrenched jobs. Tara Jollie, who had spent her professional career as a government employee, was appointed by Sarah to a position in the Department of Labor. She encountered opposition from civil servants to the changes Sarah wanted to make. "I could see who was working and who wasn't. They wanted me out." Joey Austerman worked in the state Department of Commerce and was met with a similar response. Although he worked with many dedicated, highly qualified colleagues, he saw many state employees who spent their days marking time and waiting for the next administration to arrive.

Some of those employees had genuine differences of opinion about how to get things done. Others simply didn't share the passion Sarah had for working as hard as possible to better our state. From that standpoint, she would have been better off firing all the top-level administrators and starting over, but the short window between election and inauguration meant there was little time to prepare. She had to address key appointive positions, choose the best people she could find to fill those positions, and move forward.

In spite of the difficulties she and her administration faced, Sarah was determined to keep everyone focused on the task at hand. Perhaps in a version of the coaching tactics she'd learned while playing basketball, or maybe just from her own inspiration, she found practical ways to keep her staff focused on the present. One of the things she did was to install a digital clock in the lobby of the governor's office in Anchorage. Rather than ticking forward, counting off the seconds and minutes as they passed, this clock moved backward, counting down the minutes left in her first term. Like the clock at a basketball game, it provided a very tangible reminder to everyone in the office that time was ticking and they needed to make the most out of every minute.

Hard work and long hours didn't just apply to staff and administration officials. Sarah imposed the same regimen on herself, too. More than once we received late-night replies to our e-mail messages, sometimes as late as one or two in the morning. I have no idea how she functioned so well on so little sleep. Todd, as the state's "first gentleman," devoted long hours to special projects too.

Working with Click Bishop, the commissioner of the state Department of Labor, Todd concentrated on expanding Alaska's trained workforce. He and Click worked to create a vocational training program for Alaskan students who were not planning to attend college. They also targeted dropouts. Roughly 25 percent of Alaska's high school students leave school before completing the requirements for graduation. Todd wanted to address that issue and provide training to those students.

With Sarah and Todd setting the example, members of the administration focused on the four primary areas outlined earlier in the campaign. Even though her term was cut short, they still accomplished most of what she'd wanted to do. Their formula for success was simple: work hard, use common sense, consult with real experts, do the right thing, and never forget that you are working for the people. That philosophy not only led to a successful administration, it made Sarah one of the most popular governors in the nation.

Throughout her term as governor, Sarah sought to engage the public on the issues that faced the state. She became a student of oil and gas development, both from a policy perspective and an economic perspective, and encouraged the public to learn about those topics. Alaska sits atop huge reserves of natural gas, much of which has never been developed. Constructing a pipeline to the lower forty-eight states would open a vast new source of revenue for the state and help ensure our economic future. To help Alaskans understand the importance of a new gas line to Alaska's economy, she created a page on the governor's website that included information about the issue. Videos on that site periodically updated the public on proposed legislation with details about each point. In those webcasts, she took complex economic models and made them easily understandable. That website proved effective in educating voters and politicians and helped pave the way for approval by the legislature of the gasline concept. Interestingly, when President Obama faced opposition to his proposed financial bailout legislation, he borrowed from Sarah's experience and established a website where he sought to explain to voters the details of his very complex position.

Passage of the Alaska Gasline Inducement Act, the bill that created the legislative and business context for construction of the gas pipeline, was a major achievement for Sarah's administration and for Alaska. Governors and state officials had been trying for three decades to find a way to transport natural gas from Prudhoe Bay to markets in the lower forty-eight states. Sarah set the machinery in motion to accomplish that goal by building a bipartisan coalition to guide the necessary legislation through the legislative process. With her strategic help, the bill was enacted without major changes to the provisions.

One of the things that made her popular with Alaskans was the fact that Sarah was not a "knee-jerk" conservative. She had a very down-to-earth, realistic view of her conservative values and a surprisingly broad view of the way government should operate. The breadth of her approach became obvious with the way she handled social issues, among them same-sex marriage.

In 1998, Alaskan voters adopted an amendment to the state constitution that defined marriage as a union between one man and one woman. Sarah agreed with the Judeo-Christian view of marriage and supported the 1998 amendment. During her term as governor, a gay-rights group sued the state over state-provided benefits. The state gave spousal benefits to spouses of state employees who were in heterosexual marriages, but denied those benefits to spouses of same-sex couples. At trial, the court ruled in favor of the state but on appeal, the Alaska Supreme Court overturned the lower court's order, finding that the denial of benefits to same-sex couples violated the state constitution's equal protection provision. In an attempt to counter that decision, the legislature passed a bill that prohibited the state from providing the benefits. When the bill reached Sarah's desk, she sought advice about what to do.

The attorney general and others in her administration advised her that the law was illegal. Signing it would only lead to protracted litigation, at the state's expense, and, in the end, the state would lose on appeal. Many politicians and family-values advocates wanted Sarah to sign the bill and use the resulting fight to showcase their positions on the same-sex-marriage issue. Sarah would have none of it. She wasn't interested in wasting the state's time or money grandstanding on an issue that benefited no one.

As a result, she vetoed the legislation. Not many conservative politicians would have had the guts to do that. I was proud of her for standing up for what she thought was right when others were pressuring her to do something else.

Sarah took a similar approach to the question of state vouchers for private education. She reviewed the issue, found the voucher proposals to be contrary to the state constitution, and refused to support the program. She wasn't opposed to amending the constitution to allow it, if Alaskans thought it was necessary, but she had no desire to ram legislation through the political process merely to score points with conservative advocates. As I have said before, Sarah had little patience for waste, whether it was wasted time, money, or political capital. She's been that way all her life. Not all conservatives agreed with her approach, and while she was governor she was sometimes vilified by right-wing groups as not being "conservative enough." Those accusations had no effect on Sarah's policy positions and did little to dissuade her from following her political instincts on the issues. She always had a clear sense of right and wrong. That ethos guided her through the maze of issues she encountered during her term in office. It helped her make good decisions, but it didn't make life easy for her.

In the spring of 2009, Congress enacted the Obama administration's economic stimulus package, which included large payments of federal funds to the states. Alaska was set to receive more than $930 million in direct assistance. About 30 percent of that amount was designated to pay for additional government employees in the state school system. Sarah looked over the federal legislation and found it nothing more than an attempt to grow the size of government. Accepting the money meant also accepting the programs to which the payments were assigned. Once the stimulus payments ceased, the state would be responsible for continuing to fund the programs. Sarah was concerned about the welfare of Alaskans, but she wasn't interested in merely increasing the size of the state government. As a result, she turned down about one-third of the proposed funds.

A special legislative session was called to address her decision to reject the money. Many legislators argued that if Alaska didn't accept the money, someone else would. Sen. Fred Dyson defended Sarah's decision and likened accepting the money to buying a stolen television from someone on the street. You might be getting a great deal on the TV, but that didn't make it right. Someone was going to get hurt by your "great deal." Too many people were under the impression that the stimulus money was free money when, in fact, it came at the expense of US taxpayers. It took a lot of courage for Senator Dyson and Sarah to take a stand against the federal aid. In the end, Sarah's veto on accepting the funds was overturned. I think subsequent events have shown that was a mistake and served only to push our country further into debt without providing much relief.

In the days following the 2008 campaign, the media had a field day with anything that pertained to Sarah. They constantly hounded her and members of her administration, looking for interviews and responses to their questions. When they actually landed an interview, they took the answers they received and twisted them to support whatever they had already determined to write. Almost all of the articles portrayed her in a negative light. Nothing made that more apparent than the articles written about her following the death of former governor Walter Hickel.

Hickel had been born in Kansas but moved to Alaska in the 1940s. He made a fortune in real-estate development and became a driving force in Alaska's push for statehood. In 1966, he was elected as the state's second governor. Two years later, President

Nixon appointed him Secretary of the Interior. That job took him to Washington for a while, but he returned later to serve a second term as governor. Hickel was widely popular throughout the state and had a powerful influence on Sarah's political life. He had big ideas and always tried to put Alaskans first. When she ran for governor, he was one of the few established Republicans who supported her campaign. He died in Anchorage on May 7, 2010, at the age of ninety. The funeral was held at Our Lady of Guadalupe, a Catholic church on Wisconsin Street. Sarah attended the service with Bristol and Piper.

In an effort to avoid the spotlight, Sarah arrived just as the funeral service began and sat at the back of the church. At the end of the service, as she was walking to her car, she met up with Chuck Jr. and Jeff Wheaton. As the three of them spoke, Sean Parnell, our sitting governor, came over to greet Sarah. Jeff remembered, "We were all seated in different places inside the church and only met outside afterward. Sarah was about to leave when Governor Parnell stopped to speak to her. And then the reporters began to circle around."

One of the reporters asked Sarah about what Hickel had meant to her and to our state. Sarah was very cordial and answered everything that was asked of her. The following day when newspaper articles appeared about her attendance at the service, they said Sarah had shown up at the funeral in an effort to steal the spotlight from Hickel and his grieving family. The church was packed with politicians and businessmen, including the current governor; the mayor of Anchorage; former governors Frank Murkowski, Tony Knowles, and Bill Sheffield; and former senator Ted Stevens, just to name a few. Every living person who'd ever held a position of power or influence in Alaska was there. But the press singled out Sarah as the one who was there for personal attention. That's how ridiculous the media had become and the stories they told about her were readily accepted by the public as the truth.

Jeff Wheaton remembered talking to a woman in Florida, long after the 2008 campaign. "When she found out I was from Alaska, she asked me about Sarah Palin and what I thought of her. I told her Sarah was a friend of mine. She just shook her head and scoffed, 'Never mind,' then walked away. She didn't want to hear the truth." No one did. They'd been fed a story by the news media and that's all they wanted to hear.

I was just your average hockey mom
and signed up for the PTA because
I wanted to make my kids' public
education better.

Sarah Palin

CHAPTER 17

The Nomination

A few minutes later, I watched in amazement as Sarah,
Todd, and their children emerged from the shadows and
walked to center court of the Wright State basketball arena.
CHUCK HEATH JR.

I n August 2008, Sarah and Todd showed up unexpectedly in
my classroom at Gladys Wood Elementary School in Anchorage. Sarah had visited the school a few times before and I'd taken
groups of students to the governor's office. Usually, she gave
me a heads-up before visiting but this time she just popped in
unannounced.

She arrived shortly before noon and after greeting my students we walked together into the cafeteria. The room was alive
with students busily getting their lunch and visiting with their
friends. Moments after we entered, someone noticed Sarah, and
then they all started screaming, "It's Governor Palin!"

Sarah made the rounds, shaking hands with the kids and
saying hello to as many as she could reach. Todd stood to one
side, watching. I couldn't help but notice he had a knowing grin.
Most of the time, he has a serious, no-nonsense demeanor. That
he was smiling piqued my curiosity about their visit so I asked
him, "What's up, Todd?" The tone of my voice made it more of

a statement than a question. "Why the big smile and the surprise visit?"

"Oh, no big deal." He shrugged, still grinning. "We're on our way to the airport and Sarah just wanted to say hello to your students." I asked him where they were going and he vaguely mentioned something about a meeting in Arizona. There was more to the story than "just a meeting" but I let the matter drop.

The next day, I sent Sarah an e-mail and told her, "I'm pretty sure Tim Pawlenty is going to be announced tomorrow as McCain's running mate."

"Hmmm," she replied. "I'll bet you a mocha on that."

Her response intrigued me. "You know something, don't you?" In typical Sarah fashion, she never answered that question, which meant she *did* know something, but I had no inkling what that something might be.

The next morning, Friday, August 29, I was awakened from a deep sleep by a phone call from my mother saying, "There's a rumor floating around that Sarah may be announced today as Senator McCain's running mate."

My mother was well connected to her family and kept abreast of developments in the lives of her children, grandchildren, nieces, and nephews. But when it came to politics, she had no better sources than the rest of us. Whatever she heard about John McCain and Sarah, I knew it came from one of the morning television shows. The nation's political news centers—New York and Washington, DC—are located in the Eastern time zone, which meant they were four hours later than Alaska. Morning news reports from network studios arrived in Alaska without delay, but with the time difference that was still long before sunrise. My mother and father were early risers.

"It's just a rumor," I mumbled to myself as I went back to bed.

Fifteen minutes later, I got another phone call. "Get up now and look at the television," Mom said. I still didn't think it was more than a rumor but she was insistent so I rolled out of bed and waddled into the living room, rubbing my eyes and trying to get myself awake. A few steps into the room, I stopped yawning. I was wide-awake.

On the screen, commentators and reporters I'd watched for years were busy speculating that my little sister was about to be named by John McCain as his running mate. I made my way to the sofa and took a seat. A few minutes later, the newscast switched to live footage from the arena at Wright State University in Dayton, Ohio. John McCain stood before a packed crowd and in dramatic fashion explained the qualities that made his vice presidential running mate such a compelling choice. As he ticked off the characteristics I thought to myself, *That could be Sarah.* But it could also have been any number of people.

Then, as he continued to describe his nominee, my heart rate quickened. Before long it became obvious he was going to nominate a woman, and I had a growing sense that it was Sarah. Finally, when he could wait no longer, he said with delight, "I am very pleased and very privileged to introduce to you the next vice president of the United States of America, Governor Sarah Palin of the great state of Alaska!"

I watched in amazement as Sarah, Todd, and their children emerged from the shadows and walked to center court of the arena. The rumors were true. It was official. My sister was John McCain's pick for the vice presidential nominee of the Republican Party.

Over the next few hours, reporters scrambled for information about her, piecing together tidbits from previous articles as they rushed to catch up with events. Apparently they were as unprepared for the announcement as everyone else. From the things they said, it was obvious they knew very little about her. For a while they even pronounced her name incorrectly. I just smiled and thought, *Man, she can really keep a secret.* None of us knew anything about the decision beforehand, not even Mom and Dad. Some reporters still don't believe that, but it's true. We found out about the decision with the televised announcement from Ohio, just like everyone else.

As the news shows continued, the phone began to ring. I answered the first few calls but after that I ignored them and prepared to leave for work. *Hopefully*, I thought, *I can get through my day with a normal routine and this will all go away.* I should have realized that was never going to happen.

When I arrived at school, parents of my students and most of my colleagues met me in the hall to offer congratulations. All day long they streamed into the room, asking questions, offering comments, and expressing their support for Sarah. Then someone asked when I'd be flying out to attend the Republican National Convention. In the rush of the morning and the excitement of the announcement I had thought of many things, but the idea of attending the convention had never crossed my mind. Caught up in the euphoria of the moment, I had never considered the possibility that I might actually be there in the arena when she gave her acceptance speech.

For a brief moment I thought about how wonderful that would be, then quickly dismissed the idea. The convention was scheduled for St. Paul, Minnesota, halfway across the continent. We didn't have the money for a trip like that and I didn't have time for it anyway. The school year was just beginning. My students expected me to be in class. I made it through the day and then school dismissed for the Labor Day weekend. I was glad for the extra day off on Monday and hoped some of the excitement would calm down.

The following day started as a typical Saturday. I raked leaves in the yard with the kids until midmorning. Then my sister Heather called to say that reporters had showed up on her door-step asking questions about Sarah. I had no experience with reporters and wasn't comfortable being interviewed. So I took the kids to the mall and spent most of the day away from the house.

Late that afternoon, I received a phone call from a member of John McCain's staff. Members of the campaign team wanted to meet with our extended family for a briefing. I joined them in the lobby of a nondescript Anchorage office building where we were ushered upstairs to a windowless room. In the weeks to come, the office would become known as "the Bunker." Most of the Alaska campaign work was conducted there. Right then, though, it was bare office space.

Once everyone was in place, a McCain aide entered the room and glanced around at us. "Your lives are about to change for-ever," he began. At the time, I had no idea what he meant. We all knew that Sarah's selection for the Republican ticket was a huge event, but we had not the vaguest clue about the extent to which her nomination would affect our lives.

Among the many things we were told that day was the sugges-tion that we refrain from talking to reporters unless they had been thoroughly vetted by campaign staff. "If you don't say anything, they can't twist your words and use them to hurt the campaign." I thought that advice was a little over the top. Surely no reporter would twist the truth. They might report with a perspective but they wouldn't stoop to actually fabricating news. Little did I know the eye-opening experience that awaited us all.

Looking back now, I can see we were incredibly naïve. For

one thing, none of us had a true grasp of how news reporting was deeply driven by sensationalism. Television news departments, with the demands of around-the-clock reporting, reduced complex issues to a single sound bite—usually about fifteen words in length. Reporting like that gutted a story of context and left no room for nuance. All but the most momentous events were squeezed into pithy and often glib statements designed solely to catch the viewer's attention rather than convey the truth or a clear understanding of what had transpired.

We were aware that some news organizations reported events with a slant toward a conservative or liberal perspective, depending on the channel or publication. We just didn't realize that kind of "agenda reporting" applied to us. All of us grew up with and lived among people who took us at face value. That's how we treated others and we were accustomed to being treated that way ourselves. It wasn't long before we learned that view was not correct. "Dirt," we soon realized, was at least as important to reporters as the truth, and accuracy didn't really matter at all.

Through the weekend of the initial announcement, the question my colleagues had asked earlier about whether I would attend the convention lingered in my mind. I continued to think about it and tried to calculate the cost of making the trip. Every time I did, I came to the same conclusion. There was no way we could afford it.

Then on Sunday I received a call from Todd. Sarah wanted the family with her at the convention when she gave her acceptance speech. The trip was already arranged. A jet would be waiting Tuesday morning at a private hangar in Anchorage. We were expected to board it and fly to Minnesota as guests of the McCain campaign. A private jet…the Republican Convention…that was a lifestyle far removed from my daily routine.

My sisters received the same offer but both declined. Heather was needed at home to care for her son, who couldn't travel. Her husband was needed at their newly opened business. Getting away wasn't an option for him. Molly had a scheduling conflict with her children and wouldn't be able to make the trip either. I was disappointed that they were not going, but I went to bed that night with my mind racing. Republican National Convention...private jet...my sister as nominee for vice president. Later events made me wonder if my sisters might have made the better decision. Anonymity is easier to protect than it is to recover, and nothing matters more than caring for your family. But that night, I was like a kid before Christmas. I barely slept at all.

On Monday, I realized my wardrobe lacked anything nice enough to wear to the convention, so I headed to the mall to shop for the trip. It took all of about five minutes in the major department stores to realize most of the traditional menswear brands were way beyond my price range. So I tucked my tail between my legs and retreated to a more modest store, where I found a suit that seemed just right.

Tuesday morning, we arrived at the hangar as instructed and waited while Secret Service agents checked our luggage. I had never been subjected to a security screening like that and was intrigued by the way they did their job. I'm sure my curiosity made me seem like someone who only recently wandered in from the bush, but I couldn't help myself. Those guys did a thorough job.

Once on board the airplane, the atmosphere was electric. Mom and Dad were there, along with Todd's parents and cousins from his side of the family. The plane was decorated with campaign slogans, everyone was in a great mood, and we were totally spoiled by the crew.

A few hours later we arrived in Minneapolis. The plane taxied to a stop in front of a hangar on the far side of the airport, where we were met by more campaign staff. They ushered us across the tarmac to a fleet of black SUVs and our motorcade—my first—headed downtown to the Hilton Hotel. From my window in the SUV, I could see the freeway was blocked off for us as we sped along under heavy escort.

Twenty minutes later we arrived at the hotel. We parked at an underground entrance and rode a private elevator up to our floor. After a few minutes in our rooms, everyone went downstairs to a restaurant for a private dinner and another briefing with the campaign staff. Not long after we were seated, Sarah joined us. She seemed calm and collected, which I found amazing. I would have been a wreck by then.

Later that evening, several of us attended a private book signing for Meghan McCain, who had recently authored a book about her father. The highlight of the night for me was talking with Roberta McCain, John's ninety-six-year-old mother. She was sharp, spry, and funny and told us about getting ticketed for speeding in Arizona four years earlier. She was driving 106 miles per hour at the age of ninety-two. When we left the event, she was still on the dance floor.

Wednesday morning, I awoke nervous and excited about Sarah's acceptance speech, which she would deliver later that night. I caught an early newscast that reported 89 percent of Americans had never heard of her. She truly was an unknown, both to the public and many of the political operatives within the campaign and the party. Later in the day, a speechwriter who had written for Ronald Reagan pulled me aside. He asked how I thought Sarah would do with her speech. Even he didn't know much about her. I assured him that I had seen her deliver hundreds of speeches and participate in almost as many debates. Not once had she ever failed to deliver. He nodded thoughtfully and replied, "This is a whole new ball game. This time, the entire world will be watching and the campaign might well hinge on her performance." His response hit me hard. I smiled and reassured him that she'd do fine, but inside I was suddenly more nervous than ever.

As the gravity of the moment sank in, I went to Dad's room to check on him. I wanted to make certain he understood what was about to happen. As we talked I asked him what he was going to wear that night. When he told me he was wearing an old tan sport coat—which was way too small—and dark slacks, I knew we needed help. About that time, an aide from the campaign, a young man from Texas named Seth, approached us and asked if we were all set for the night's events. I took him aside and lowered my voice. "Is there any way we could take my father shopping? His clothes need an upgrade."

Seth arranged for a car to shuttle us to a nearby Macy's store. Once there, we were greeted by a personal shopper, who took us straight to the suit department. Dad and I were both fitted with new suits. We never could have afforded clothes like that, but were assured that the cost was a legitimate campaign expense that the campaign would bear. As most of America knows by now, when news reporters learned about the shopping trip they wrote a series of scathing articles suggesting we had demanded new clothes and then had taken advantage of the situation with a shopping spree. Nothing could have been further from the truth. We were just two guys trying to navigate a lifestyle as foreign to us as life on the opposite side of the world. Had we known that what the aides offered us was somehow wrong, we would have refused on the spot.

After we returned to the hotel I put the clothes in my room

and rode down to the lobby. There was too much happening to waste time lounging around. I spent the remainder of the day walking through the convention exhibit halls with our parents. No one knew us. The only odd thing people may have noticed were the mysterious men wearing suits, sunglasses, and earpieces, shadowing our every move.

That evening at the convention center, I watched in awe as Sarah took the stage. She was my little sister, but there she was, a contender in a presidential election with an honest shot at becoming the next vice president. I wanted to think of all the things that had happened to us—growing up in Alaska, the people we'd known, and the events that shaped us—but right then all I could think of was how very proud I was to see her and to be a small part of her success.

The speech started slowly, but about ten minutes into it she hit her stride. Words that began at a labored pace suddenly took on power and a force of their own. I scanned the crowd and noticed people actually sitting on the edge of their seats, straining to hear every word she said. I've watched a video of the speech many times since, and the recordings never do it justice. That evening, with Sarah at center stage, was incredible.

A few minutes before Sarah concluded, we were guided from our seats and led backstage. We watched the end of the speech on monitors in the green room. The original plan was for our entire family to walk onto the stage as she finished and congratulate her. Twice, we made it to the edge of the stage only to be pulled back as the crowd's response continued. Then suddenly, John McCain appeared and excitedly rushed out ahead of us. We were disappointed not to appear before the crowd. Most of us had told our friends and family at home to watch for us at the end, but we were also relieved and happy with Sarah's strong performance.

After the applause subsided, Sarah joined us in the green room. For someone thrust into the limelight not even a week earlier, she seemed amazingly calm and collected. I asked her if she had been nervous while she was onstage and she replied, "I was just excited to share my message."

Seconds later, McCain burst into the room and threw his arms around Sarah. "Unbelievable!" he exclaimed. "That was great. Just terrific! I'm blown away, Sarah. I never could have pulled that off." His comments seemed a little strange, but then we learned about the problem with the teleprompter that forced Sarah to improvise and deliver most of her remarks from memory.

When we returned to the hotel, Sarah, Todd, and most of the family went to their rooms. It was late in the evening but I was too excited to sleep. Instead, Dad and I went down to the lobby to see if we could gauge the reaction of attendees to the speech. When people recognized us as Sarah's relatives, we were mobbed with congratulations. Everyone kept repeating, "She knocked it out of the park!" The mood was boisterous and festive. Sarah had breathed new life into the campaign and the crowd was in a mood to celebrate.

As we worked the room, people kept asking where Sarah was and whether she would join us. After several people made the same comment, Dad told me to go up to her room and get her. So I headed back to our floor. When I knocked on Sarah's door, she answered in her pajamas. She had been lounging on a sofa, having a snack and casually watching the news. I told her that the lobby was packed with people who were begging for a chance to congratulate her. She said, "Give me a minute to change."

Then Todd intervened. "Chuck, there's no way she's going down there. We've got a super-early flight to catch to Wisconsin and she needs to sleep."

Sarah heard him and called in reply, "Todd, I'm going." I had heard that tone in her voice before and I knew there was nothing he could do to stop her. Members of her Secret Service detail tried to stop her too, arguing that they had not planned for an excursion of that nature and that security would be impossible. Sarah said simply, "I'm going." And out the door we went with the agents in tow. Then, as we approached the elevator, she leaned near to me and said, "Chuck, I hope you realize that this is the last time I'll ever be able to do something like this." I didn't understand what she meant at the time. I do now.

When the elevator doors opened in the lobby, Sarah stepped out and was immediately surrounded. I had heard of rock stars being mobbed by their adoring fans, but that was the first time I'd witnessed it firsthand. People were so excited to see her and to get close to her they could barely contain themselves. As they pressed closer, Sarah grabbed my coattail and I pulled her into the lounge, where Dad and a group of McCain's old friends were waiting. Pictures were taken, hugs were given, more words of encouragement and congratulations were shared, and thirty minutes later, Sarah said, "You better get me out of here." Before I could react, the Secret Service agents surrounded her and rushed her back to her room.

Many people that evening thanked us for the huge sacrifice we and our families were making. I thought that was an odd comment at the time. What sacrifice? We were having a ball, traveling, meeting incredible people, and being the focus of so much attention. Where was the sacrifice? We would find out soon enough.

The night finally wound down and we all headed to bed feeling confident that the election was going to go our way. That next day as we prepared to return home, I saw John McCain's brother,

Joe, in the hotel. "We've got it in the bag!" I chortled. He gave me a serious look and shook his head. "You have no idea what they're about to do to your sister."

His remark caught me off guard. I was certain Sarah's speech had turned the tide of the campaign and I told him so. "The speech was a tremendous help," he replied. "But the Democrats and the media will do their best to tear her apart." As I was soon to see, his warning was an understatement.

God, you always said you would
not give us something we could
not handle. I think you might have
overestimated us.

Sarah Palin

CHAPTER 18

A Life That Matters

There were things I needed to say—things I wanted to
say—and suddenly the time seemed too short.
CHUCK HEATH SR.

Our good friend Mary Ellan Moe once said, "Children humble you. They teach you things you don't learn anywhere else." That was true of our children. They taught me things I never would have learned anywhere else. Some of those lessons—like the warmth of unconditional love and the strength of familial camaraderie—reached deep into my life, generations deep, in fact. The bond we shared as a family and the commitment we forged brought me to a place of resolution that I don't think I would have found any other way.

My sister, Carol, two years older than I, was born prematurely. She had a twin sister who was stillborn. When Carol came home from the hospital to our house in North Hollywood, my parents took turns with her lying on their chest. After a few days, they moved her to her first crib, which was a shoebox. She was incredibly small. At times, they brought her to the kitchen and set her in the shoebox on the open door of the oven to keep her warm. As she grew, they moved her from the shoebox to a dresser drawer.

Carol suffered from birth with infantile paralysis, which left her physically impaired. However, she refused to cower to her physical limitations and did her best to lead a normal life. She tried to play with the other kids and do all the things the rest of us were doing, but many of the kids in the neighborhood teased her about her condition. I had numerous fistfights defending her honor.

We had been close through most of our childhood and into our high school years, but as my relationship with our parents deteriorated, Carol and I grew further apart. After we graduated from Sandpoint High, she moved to California and married. I did not attend the wedding. She and her husband, Gordon, visited us once in Alaska and that was the last time I saw her.

As an adult, she overcame many of her physical limitations and lived a rich and rewarding life. She was a kind and gentle woman whose indomitable spirit was an example of perseverance and determination. I should have told her how much she meant to me, but I didn't. Then, at the age of forty-two, she succumbed to cancer. I remember the day Gordon called to tell us she had died. When he delivered the news, I wept.

After I learned Carol's husband did not plan to have a funeral for her, I decided to remain in Alaska rather than travel to Los Angeles where she lived. "I hadn't seen her in years," I told myself. "What good would traveling there do now that she was dead?" I sent money to cover the cost of cremation, but I lived to regret not going there and often wished I had handled the situation differently. Not just her death, but my relationship with her in general. I should have stayed in contact with her and told her how much I admired her.

Maybe it was the realization that losing my relationship with Carol was a tragedy. Or, as I have already suggested, that our children and the love I shared with them changed me. It might have been all those prayers they prayed for me after Mary Ellan took Sally to church that Saturday and their lives became more oriented toward faith in God. For whatever reason, in the years following Carol's death I slowly came to realize that perhaps I had judged my father too harshly that summer before my junior year in high school—when we had the fight about sports and I left home. I was young and headstrong. He had seemed selfish, less interested in my future than he was in the past. Nothing excited him more than to entertain his friends with stories about the places he'd been, the people he'd seen, and the thrilling adventures he'd had along the way. As I grew older I realized I was a lot like him in that respect. I had come to love a good story, especially the ones I told, and often in the midst of a good one I could hear his voice coming from my lips.

In January 1980, my mother called to tell me my father had suffered a severe heart attack. He was in a hospital in Yuma, Arizona, a town where they went during the winter months to escape the cold of northern Idaho. His heart had been critically damaged. The doctors didn't give him long to live. If I wanted to see him before he died, I'd better come quickly.

The news hit me hard. There were things I needed to say—things I wanted to say—and suddenly the time seemed too short. Sally and I threw some clothes in a suitcase and prepared to leave that night.

This was in the days before ATMs and debit cards. Credit cards, though widely available, were still used far less than cash for most transactions. We used cash for just about everything, but it required planning and time to get to the bank to make a withdrawal. As we prepared to leave, I realized I was running low on cash.

That fall, Chuck Jr. had entered his senior year at Wasilla High School. He played on the football team, but in Alaska football season starts in the middle of the summer in order to play the games before the nights become unbearably cold. After football season ends, they play basketball. At a time when most students in the lower forty-eight states are seated in the bleachers cheering their teams through the latter stages of the football season, Alaska students are in the gym. Chuck Jr. played on the Wasilla team.

One of the highlights that year was a trip to Hawaii, where the team participated in a tournament. The trip offered them a chance to get away from the Alaskan winter for a few days and gave them the opportunity to play against teams from other parts of the nation. All that fall, members of the Wasilla team worked hard to raise money for the expense of that trip. I made the trip with them as a chaperone.

We had a great time and returned just a few days before my mother called to tell me about my father. Chuck Jr. still had money left from the trip. If I wanted to see my father before he died, I would have to ask my son for a loan to help cover the cost. Mary Ellan was right—children have a way of humbling you. Chuck Jr. was glad to loan me the money. That part was affirming, but the irony of the moment was not lost on me. The relationship my father and I had drove us apart. The relationship Chuck Jr. and I enjoyed drew us closer together.

With Chuck Jr.'s help, Sally and I made it to Yuma that night. We rented a car and rode out to the trailer where my parents had been living that winter. Mom wasn't there, so we drove to the hospital. As I came into the room I found my father lying in bed. He had tubes in his arms and an oxygen mask over his face. I wasn't sure how he would receive me. A lot had happened since the days when I palled around Los Angeles with him—me just a little boy, him very much an adult. Remembering those days and seeing him in that hospital bed made the moment all the more real. Those lighter days of old were never coming back. The most I could hope for was to find peace between us.

We talked that evening and I learned that asking me to come down there had been his idea. He wanted to talk, and in our conversation he apologized for many of the things he'd done—the backhanded slaps, beatings with a rubber hose, and the way he'd reacted to my interest in sports. Most of all, he apologized for the ultimatum that drove a wedge between us all those many years ago. I forgave him and admitted I could have handled the situation differently myself. Then he apologized to my mother for being so domineering. I had never seen him treat her in an unkind manner, but he didn't make much room for her either.

That evening, sitting there around his bed, all the years of separation melted away. The walls that the three of us had built that separated us crumbled and fell. For those few hours that evening it was almost like we were back in North Hollywood, tramping from event to event, him with his camera and me at his side.

Later that evening, we drove Mom back to the trailer and spent the night with her. The next morning when we arrived at the hospital we learned that Dad had passed away.

A few months after his death we gathered on a dock at Pend Oreille Landing, a marina just down the road from the house in Hope, Idaho. Dad enjoyed many hours in the café there, telling those stories he loved to tell. It was a sunny, pleasant day and we spent a few minutes remembering him, our memories now tempered by the release we'd found shortly before he died. Then, after a prayer and a few remarks, I poured his ashes into the lake, just as he'd requested. As the ashes drifted away with the gentle lapping of the waves, the pain of my past quietly drifted away too.

Psychologists say that unresolved conflict ties us to the pain of our past. In a very real sense, reconciling with my father unchained me from the things that had transpired between us. I still remember what happened, but now I see it for what it was—two men who struggled with their relationship, parted company, and found each other again. Some people call that closure. I think of it as perspective.

Those same psychologists also suggest that a son takes the agenda for his life from the unfinished agenda of his father. That may be true. My father wanted to get away from the urban lifestyle of Los Angeles and pursue life in rural America. Though he'd lived in Los Angeles all his life, he saw himself as a man of the outdoors and did his best to work our small farm, fish the lake, and hunt the mountains that surrounded our home. In truth, he wasn't very good at any of those tasks. He was an excellent photographer, but milking a cow or tending the pigs wasn't the best use of his talent.

If it is true that I obtained my agenda from him, then I fulfilled it to the fullest. I've hunted and fished my way from Idaho to the northern shores of the Alaska mainland, miles above the Arctic Circle. I've trapped varmints from Staten Island in New York City to the Aleutian Islands on the opposite end of the continent and on Palmyra, way out in the Pacific Ocean. Since retiring from teaching, Sally and I have been to several big game preserves in Africa and we've seen the wilds of China. When it comes to fulfilling the dream of living an outdoor life, we've done it, and we brought our children along for most of that journey.

Chuck Jr., Heather, Sarah, and Molly were shaped by my fascination with hunting, trapping, fishing, and exploring the mountains around us. There was no way for them to avoid it. We took them into the woods almost every weekend. Each of them learned to shoot a rifle, bait a trap, skin and butcher an animal. They were shaped by those experiences, but not all of them embraced the outdoor life. What they did embrace was the underlying ethos.

At the heart of my father's quest, and at the heart of my own journey, was a desire to live a life of meaning, a life that counts. To really "do it," whatever the "it" was. For me, meaning came from doing. Whatever sense of "being" I had was defined by action. I got that from my father. For him, it was never enough to call yourself a photographer. You had to actually take photographs. You couldn't just call yourself a fisherman, you had to actually get out on the lake and fish. I took it another step further. For me, I had to do it *better* than everyone else, and it was the same with hunting, trapping, sports, and all our other endeavors.

I did not intentionally set out to make my children outdoor enthusiasts. My goal was to make them into productive adults. Because hunting, fishing, and enjoying the outdoors was what I was already doing, I used those endeavors to teach them about life. The intensity of the quest just came along with the quest.

In the larger sense, that underlying drive for "really doing it" compelled Chuck Jr. to take a leave of absence from teaching to spend a year mining for gold. Panning for it on weekends as a casual hobby would never be enough. Just as merely participating in a sport was never enough. Our family ethos required dedication, commitment, and work.

That same drive also explains why Heather was more interested in coming back to Alaska to work with children rather than pursuing an academic life. She wanted to "do it," not just talk about it. And she did. After she graduated, she took a job teaching in the bush. Molly was driven by the same motivation.

With Sarah, it was never enough to simply hold a political idea as an abstract thought. She had to "do something." For her, politics was never about simply "being." It was always about "doing." When she saw a chance to make a difference in Wasilla, she stepped forward and ran for the seat on the city council. That was part of the reason she got into the lieutenant governor's race too. I know that's why she sought the governor's office and why she agreed to serve as John McCain's running mate. It wasn't about the glamour or the publicity. It was about the opportunity to make a difference and to actually be the person she'd always wanted to be—a person whose life mattered.

Our children obtained that agenda from us—from Sally and me, and from all the others you've read about—Clem, Charlie, and hundreds of others. I'm not an introspective guy, and we're not an introspective family. Writing this book is about the most introspective I've been in my life, but I think I'm correct. And if I'm correct, that I received from Charlie the unfinished agenda of finding a life that really mattered, then that was the greatest gift of all and the kindest thing he ever did for me.

Buck up, or stay in the truck.

Sarah Palin

CHAPTER 19

The 2008 Campaign

No one was looking for "feel-good" stories on Sarah.
They wanted sensational scandal.
CHUCK HEATH JR.

The day after we returned from the convention I went back to work and was greeted by students and fellow teachers who wanted to hear about the trip. During my planning period that day I put together a PowerPoint presentation with pictures of our experiences and announced that I'd be sharing it in the library after classes ended that afternoon. When school dismissed, I gathered my things and walked down there. I assumed about a dozen people would show up. Then I opened the door and found the room was full. Teachers and staff were crammed into every available space. As I made my way through the presentation, they sat with rapt attention, hanging on every word, taking in every detail of every photograph.

The next few weeks were crazy. Our home phone rang constantly with calls from friends and reporters. Television stations and newspapers from around the country wanted an interview— even people from a few foreign countries too. We turned down almost every one because that's what the campaign had instructed us to do. Mom and Dad got hit the hardest. In one day alone, they received 327 phone calls, 81 from reporters requesting interviews. Some of the questions, like, "Did your family ever live in an igloo?" showed just how little most people knew about us and about life in Alaska.

A number of reporters tried to coerce us into giving interviews by telling us things like, "If you don't provide us with an interview or a quote, we'll go to one of the wackos out there who are happy to talk trash about Sarah and we'll print their quotes instead." That was probably the most difficult thing to handle because it put us in a really awkward position. If we refused to talk, they would print something outlandish from the least credible "sources" they could find. But if we relented and talked, they often edited our responses in a way that converted something we meant as a positive comment into a negative statement. Sometimes they lifted quotes from the answer to one question and used them as if they were an assertion made in a different context. Even when they got the facts straight, they frequently attributed the information to the wrong source.

One day, I received a call from a friend who was working as a barista in a coffee shop in Wasilla. The shop was crawling with reporters and she overheard one talking to a high school student. The reporter, who was from Los Angeles, had pulled the kid in from the sidewalk and offered him cash to provide any "dirt" he had on the Palins. He was specifically looking for information about Track and Bristol, Sarah's eldest children. According to our friend, the reporter had been working other kids the same way all morning.

Along with the hundreds of reporters that descended on the town came teams of investigators from the Barack Obama campaign. They were there solely for opposition research—an all-out, no-holds-barred attempt to obtain damaging information that could be used to smear Sarah's character and ruin her reputation. Often defended as necessary for a candidate and helpful for the public—by providing the public with useful information as voters make their voting decisions—opposition research is historically a sinister operation, gathering information from any and every source possible, regardless of whether that information is obtained by legal means. In that effort, campaign researchers often work hand-in-hand with reporters for the sole purpose of destroying the candidacy of one rival or another. No one was looking for "feel-good" stories on Sarah. They wanted sensational scandal.

A reporter from the *New York Times* contacted Jerry Yates, Sarah's junior high basketball coach, hoping to get an appointment for an interview with someone who'd known Sarah a long time. Jerry, wanting to help as much as possible, agreed to talk. Then he said, "But if you're looking for something about Sarah that's off-color, don't bother coming." The reporter never showed for the interview. Jerry remembered, "None of us were ready to see her slaughtered like she was by the media after she went outside [Alaska] to run with McCain."

Don Moore, who worked as borough manager when Sarah served on the city council and as mayor, was asked by a national reporter about books Sarah had supposedly banned from the library. When he told the reporter no books were banned, she hung up on him.

When reporters didn't find what they were looking for from our family and friends, they turned to anyone with the slightest connection to us, many of whom we'd never known. Using any means necessary, reporters scoured the Alaskan countryside until they obtained the quotes that fit their version of what Sarah and our family were "really" like. And it wasn't happening only in Alaska. Stories came from every direction and almost none of them were true.

I remember watching a YouTube clip of Matt Damon shaking his head in disgust and saying that he could never vote for Sarah who, according to him, was a "book banner" and one who believed dinosaurs walked the earth as recently as four thousand years ago. Damon went on to say that because she spoke in folksy terms, was only the mayor of a small city, and governed a state like Alaska, there was no way Sarah was fit for the White House. He delivered his statement with sincerity—I'm sure he actually believed what he said—then newscasters took that sincerity and sold it as an indication that Damon's statements contained factual accuracy. In fact, his statements could not have been more incorrect. Sarah never banned or attempted to ban any book in any library and she never said anything about how recently dinosaurs lived on earth.

During the campaign, Tina Fey further bolstered her comedic career by lampooning Sarah on the television show *Saturday Night Live*. Her portrayal of Sarah produced the most famous misquote of the entire campaign: "I can see Russia from my house." Sarah never said that, either. In an interview, she had said, while illustrating Alaska's proximity to Russia, "There are places in Alaska where you can actually see Russia." Even a lot of our friends confused the Tina Fey quote with Sarah's actual words because Fey's remarks were so widely reported. There are places in Alaska where Russia is well within eyesight. Little Diomede Island is only two and a half miles from the Russian island of Big Diomede. In 1987, Lynne Cox, an American open-water swimmer, swam the channel between the islands. On a clear day, Wales, Alaska, located on the western tip of the Seward Peninsula, affords a view of the Russian coastline and mountains. But no one cared about that. They just accepted the lie as the truth and believed what they were told.

When the 2008 campaign ended in a loss, the same process of bending, shaping, and fabricating the facts repeated itself even among those associated with the campaign. No one on the McCain staff wanted to take responsibility for the strategic decisions, many of which had been made before Sarah was brought on board, that contributed to their defeat. Instead, they did their best to lay that responsibility at Sarah's feet. She had been a participant in the campaign for a little more than two months. Others had been involved for almost two years. Yet somehow they wanted everyone to believe that the loss was Sarah's fault. In fact, the opposite was true.

The week before John McCain announced the selection of his running mate, he trailed Barack Obama in the polls 47 percent to 43 percent. Democrats and many Independents were energized by the prospect of electing the first African American to the presidency of the United States. Momentum was on their side and they had a huge fund-raising lead. The Republican Party's decision to nominate Sarah to the 2008 ticket turned that around.

The McCain-Palin campaign came out of the Republican National Convention leading in most major opinion polls by a margin of 50 percent to 46 percent. That McCain had a legitimate possibility of winning, even right up to Election Day, had more to do with Sarah than anything the campaign staff attempted. Unfortunately, in the days following the election, none of that stopped campaign staff members, consultants, and strategists from lining up for interviews to give their so-called "unbiased" opinions about what went wrong with the campaign. Those opinions focused on supposed mistakes Sarah made in a blatant attempt to shift the post-election discussion away from the McCain staff's failure to adequately capitalize on the renewed energy Sarah brought to the campaign.

To make matters worse, many who gave those self-serving interviews attempted to buttress their opinions with versions of the facts that suited their purposes rather than conveying the truth. We had come to expect this sort of thing from Democrats—they had been fictionalizing the truth about Sarah since she entered the campaign. But to have Republican operatives and consultants, who were supposed to be fellow conservatives, engage in the same kind of activity seemed all the more reprehensible, especially coming from those who were instrumental in reaching the decisions and in creating the problems about which they were then complaining.

All those times they mismanaged Sarah in the campaign were twisted afterward into evidence that she was indifferent, uninformed, and disinterested. Times when she pushed back and tried to assert herself were remade into evidence that she was difficult to work with or prone to tantrums. They couldn't bear the thought of acknowledging that she had political instincts at least equal to their own and a win-loss record far better than that of even the most senior McCain campaign consultants. In fact, most of the senior staff's only winning experience came in the 2004 reelection of George W. Bush, where they had the decided advantage of campaigning as the incumbent. That they undermined their own efforts for the McCain-Palin ticket became obvious when at least one of those inner-circle advisers later admitted not even voting for them. That same process of straining the truth to the point of incredulity continues today as people affiliated with both parties reconfigure the facts about Sarah through books, novels, and movies that serve only their personal interests.

Early in the campaign, as the systemic nature of those attacks first began to emerge, Kris Perry, who was by then administrative director in the governor's Anchorage office, and Sarah sought a way to counter the erroneous accounts being generated in the press. To do that, they turned to Meghan Stapleton.

Two years into her job as Sarah's press secretary, Meghan gave birth to her first child. Not long after that, she left her job and went home to be a mother. When John McCain asked Sarah to join him on the Republican ticket, Meghan was working from home as a communications consultant on the gasline issue. Sarah and Kris asked her to help with the campaign. "A two-month sprint," they said. "We need you."

Meghan agreed to help the McCain-Palin campaign staff for what everyone thought would be a short stint of aggressive news coverage, after which the work would become more manageable. A week later, it was obvious the thousands of reporters who had arrived in Alaska weren't going home anytime soon. Meghan, with her knowledge of the issues and personalities involved in the questions they were raising, proved indispensable in responding to what became a very negative and destructive media war against all things Sarah.

On October 2, 2008, Sarah had her first and only debate with Joe Biden. Similar to our reaction before the convention speech, we were nervous for her, but excited, too. Biden had thirty-five years of political service under his belt and had served in Washington, DC, for a long time. His experience made him a potentially formidable challenge, but Sarah was no rookie either. She had been involved in politics for twenty years. During her previous campaigns she had delivered innumerable speeches and had participated in debates that were at least as hotly contested as the one in which she was now engaged.

In one of her rare absences from the state during the

campaign, Meghan flew down for the debate preparation. What she found there astounded her. Aides were standing offstage shouting answers to Sarah, sometimes contradicting one another in their attempt to micromanage her responses. She had notecards they gave her that had contradictory answers on them. The resulting tension made her appear hesitant and tentative. As Meghan described her, "This was not the woman we knew." Sarah knew the topics, but in an effort to steer her answers toward a controlled, predetermined result, campaign aides were driving her away from the image that had made her an attractive candidate. Finally, Meghan and Kris Perry intervened to give Sarah time alone before the debate started.

Back in Alaska, we had a "watch party" at the home of Kristen Cole, one of Sarah's close friends. Things were going well—better than we expected—when, in the middle of the debate, Sarah gave a "shout-out" to all the students in my class at Gladys Wood Elementary School. I was certain that meant one thing—reporters would be waiting for me at school the following morning.

Sure enough, when I arrived for class the next day, thirteen news crews were at the school. A couple of them were already set up in my classroom. The kids took it well and did their best to ignore the cameras while I tried to teach.

Later in the day, my principal, Jennifer Schmitz, called me to her office. "Chuck," she began, "this is not going to work. You need to take some time off." Reluctantly, I agreed and contacted the district supervisor of elementary education about how to handle the situation. He suggested that I use something called "civic leave." I could get out on the campaign trail, keep a journal of my experiences, and share it with teachers from the district when I returned.

It sounded like a great idea—I could take advantage of a

once-in-a-lifetime opportunity, and our teachers would catch an inside view of how campaigns worked. However, when the suggestion reached the superintendent of schools, she shot it down. Instead of doing the project, I took leave without pay, which was financially painful but necessary under the circumstances.

The day after I went on leave from teaching, I started to work in the Alaska office of the McCain-Palin campaign. This was an effort arranged and staffed by the Alaska State Republican Party. They worked in conjunction with McCain's national campaign staff but the operation from that office was controlled by the state Republican Party. Randy Ruedrich, with whom Sarah had served on the Oil and Gas Conservation Commission, was still chairman of the state party and very much in control of the state party's work in promoting the McCain-Palin candidacy. Having him in charge of Sarah's political future left me very uneasy. Not only had she cited him for ethics violations while on the commission— a move that resulted in his resignation—earlier that year, in March of 2008, she had been involved in an attempt to strip him of his Republican Party leadership position. I'm sure he was as troubled by my presence as I was by his.

One of my responsibilities at the Anchorage office was to sort through the large volume of mail that arrived for Sarah. Letters came to her from all over the country. Someone had to read through them, decide which ones needed a response, and process a reply. The volume of correspondence was overwhelming. One entire office was dedicated to nothing but that task. Often the cases of mail were stacked five feet high.

One of the letters I read was from a thirteen-year-old girl from Florida named Rachel. In the letter, she talked about the death of her mother four years earlier, and how Sarah had become a powerful role model for her. Normally, we sent a preprinted thank-you note as a response, but Rachel's letter inspired me. Instead of mailing a reply, I picked up the phone and called her. Rachel's father, Don, answered. When he realized that I was Sarah's brother, he started crying. He told me how much the call would mean to Rachel but that she wasn't home.

As we talked, he mentioned that they lived near Boca Raton. Sarah was scheduled to speak at a hotel there the next night. After the call ended, I phoned Sarah and told her about Rachel. She said she'd try to give her a call. I didn't think much about it until a few days later when I received a phone call from Rachel's dad.

Not only did Sarah contact Rachel, she sent a limo to Rachel's house and brought them to the hotel where she was speaking. That event included dinner, which Rachel and her father enjoyed while seated next to Sarah. A few days later, Don sent me a front-page story from their local newspaper about the event and Rachel's experiences that night. That's how Sarah saw the campaign— an opportunity to change the country, and in the process, an opportunity to change individual lives of the people she met.

Meanwhile, Sarah was working hard to gear up for the political battle that faced her. She came to the campaign from the governor's office, where she'd been immersed in issues that directly affected Alaska. She had worked hard to develop a thorough, detailed understanding of the complex challenges that confronted the state—gasline construction, oil and gas leases, infrastructure planning and construction, and natural-resource policy. She was more than conversant on those topics. When she joined the presidential race, there were national and world issues on which she needed additional briefing. The McCain campaign made certain she received position papers on all of those issues and assigned advisers to walk her through the subject matter. One of her advisers, Charlie Black, whom we first met in St. Paul at the Republican National Convention, told me that he had advised many presidents, including Ronald Reagan, and that Sarah was by far the quickest study. According to him, she absorbed and assimilated information four times faster than George W. Bush. I don't doubt it. She was always able to distill a complicated topic down to its essential components, without losing the big-picture context.

While Sarah was coming up to speed on issues the other candidates had been discussing over the past two years, core leaders in the McCain campaign moved to control much of what she said in speeches at public rallies and in interviews given to the media. Those of us who knew her best—family, friends, and supporters in Alaska—could readily see that what she said sounded little like the person we'd known. Sarah did her best to follow the script given to her by advisers and speechwriters, but often the views she was expected to express were not positions she had "owned" as her personal preference. Neither was the language. When she gave those speeches the way advisers wanted, the audience response was muted and polite, but not enthusiastic.

Very quickly, she noticed that when she tossed aside the prepared remarks and spoke about the topics from her heart, the message resonated with the public. More and more, as the campaign continued Sarah inserted her own comments into the prepared speeches. McCain staffers referred to those improvised remarks as "going rogue." They meant it as a jibe against her but Sarah took the phrase as synonymous with speaking up for the typical American citizen. Later, she used it as the title of her first book.

What those staffers failed to realize was that the "rogue" statements were the lines from the speeches that electrified the public. Those quips and verbal jabs conveyed Sarah's passion for getting the country moving again and showed her sincerity in trying to accomplish that task while still exhibiting compassion for the dire circumstances most citizens faced. The crowds sensed her caring attitude and responded with enthusiastic support. By trying to muzzle her and keep her "on script," the McCain campaign actually worked against Sarah's greatest strengths. The confusion that resulted from their efforts to rein her in led to many of the glitches and gaffes that were so widely reported.

Sarah has a gift of being able to reach out to others and express what they are already thinking. As many of her friends noticed, while Sarah was John McCain's running mate she didn't get to do that. She didn't get to be Sarah. And that was one of the biggest issues Sarah struggled with during the campaign.

Most vice presidential candidates enter the presidential campaign at the convention, deliver a great speech to the party faithful, and provide a ratings pop for the presidential ticket. Then they recede quietly into the background and ride out the remainder of the campaign waiting for Election Day. Sarah wasn't that kind of politician. She didn't want to be "managed." I've known her all her life and trying to handle her that way only leads to confrontation. Once she's made up her mind about how something ought to be done, getting on board and helping her works much better than opposing and trying to change her with direct confrontation. Dad recognized that by the time she was two years old. I learned it as a teenager. Most people working for the McCain campaign never quite understood her. Actually, they didn't understand any of us.

After several weeks working in Anchorage with the Alaska Republican Party's effort, distributing signs, handing out bumper stickers, and answering letters, I wanted to be more involved in the national campaign. By then we knew that the McCain-Palin ticket was going to win in Alaska. In an effort to get beyond the work in our home state, I visited the Bunker, the office in the building where we were briefed by representatives from John McCain's campaign right after Sarah was announced as McCain's choice of running mate. The stated purpose of the office was to allow members of the McCain national staff to coordinate the national campaign with the state effort. In reality, the men and women who worked at the Bunker spent most of their time tirelessly countering erroneous, misleading, and false reports generated by Democratic hit squads and their colleagues in the news media.

In the course of the campaign, people working from this office became known as the Truth Squad, a moniker thrown at them in derision by mainstream news outlets but accepted as a badge of honor by Sarah's supporters. They worked fourteen to eighteen hours each day, seven days a week, monitoring radio, television, Internet, and print media in an all-out effort to make sure the American people received an accurate account of who Sarah was and what she said.

I suggested the campaign might use me better somewhere else. I didn't have any special skills as a campaign worker, but I was Sarah's brother and I thought my connection to her might have some weight with potential voters. She couldn't be everywhere at the same time and surrogates for her were in short supply. A few days later, I was reassigned to an office in Reno, Nevada.

For the remainder of the campaign, I worked in Nevada doing media interviews and events in towns across the state. The reception I received was incredible. People were grateful that a member of Sarah's family took time to meet with them. Not long after I arrived, I called Mom and Dad and suggested they join me. I knew that if crowds were greeting Sarah's brother with enthusiasm, they would be even more excited to see her mother and father. I was right, too. When they arrived, the crowds went wild. Not getting them involved earlier was a big mistake.

Our cousin Dylan Jones, a student at Eastern Washington University, took time away from school to join us. He worked from the Las Vegas and Henderson offices doing grassroots organization among eighteen- to twenty-four-year-olds. Working behind the scenes of the campaign proved to be a life-changing experience for him. After the election, he returned to school and changed his major. He also changed colleges and two years later graduated from Gonzaga University with a degree in political science.

The day after Mom and Dad arrived in Nevada, we rode over to the campaign office in Las Vegas. We were surprised to find Jerry Tarkanian working in the office. Jerry had enjoyed a long and illustrious career coaching basketball at the University of Nevada–Las Vegas (UNLV). His son, Danny, was in the office, too. Dad had followed Jerry's career for many years and was excited to actually meet him. Jerry's life had been focused on sports but he watched Sarah's speech at the Republican Convention and became enamored of her. He felt the country was headed in the wrong direction. Sarah's commonsense manner was one he could easily relate to and he was excited to find a politician who would "tell it like it is." After Sarah's speech, Jerry became politically active for the first time in his life and volunteered to work with the campaign.

Jerry wasn't the only one who responded to her with his feet. Across the country, volunteers turned out at local campaign offices. They stood on street corners and waved signs to passing motorists, knocked on doors to hand out fliers, made phone calls, passed out bumper stickers, and covered the countryside with yard signs.

That kind of passionate response was reminiscent of the reaction she drew in the 2006 governor's race, and in the campaigns she waged in Wasilla. At every level, people responded to her by getting off the sofa and heading down to the campaign office. In 2008, her involvement in the McCain-Palin campaign brought that same enthusiastic expression from supporters everywhere.

A few days later, we were invited to speak to a meeting of the UNLV Young Republicans. Dylan went with us. When we arrived on campus, we met with a group of about ten student Republicans. They were few in number but well informed on the crucial issues of the election and deeply concerned about the direction of the country. They had done their homework, too. In addition to understanding the party platform, they also knew the political backgrounds of both John and Sarah.

After talking to the Young Republicans, we walked over to the Student Union Building. It was noon and the place was filled with students who were eating lunch. Never shy about anything, Dad plunged into the crowd, introduced himself as Sarah Palin's father, and started talking. Many were shocked by his sudden, unannounced appearance, but Dad just kept smiling and talking his way across the room.

As was the case at many universities, most of the students at UNLV were Obama supporters. A number of them wore T-shirts and campaign buttons to show their interest. Their election paraphernalia was like a magnet to Dad and drew him right to them. He moved from group to group engaging them in his own friendly but direct way, usually with an opening line like, "Say hello to Sarah Palin's father!" He said it with such enthusiasm that the students were immediately disarmed.

At one table, he spoke to a female student named Addison. Like others in the crowd, she wore an Obama T-shirt. I remember her name because I had a student in my class back in Anchorage with the same name. Dad thanked her for being politically involved and then asked her why she and her fellow students were all supporting Barack Obama. She told him that they were all ready for a big change in Washington and Obama gave them hope that things would be different. "I agree with you," Dad replied. "We need some major changes in Washington." Then he asked her to tell him specifically what she thought Obama was going to change, and what he had done in the past that gave her reason to believe he was the most qualified person to bring about that change. She responded with nothing but silence. He pressed her for an answer, but she couldn't tell him a single thing about Obama's past or why he might be qualified to run the country.

As we moved through the room, students watched and craned their necks to hear what Dad was saying. Once they figured out who we were, I think they wanted a confrontation, but Dad was pleasant and respectful, which gave them little room to rant and argue. All they got was a really nice man pointing to some basic things that most of them had never stopped to consider. I don't think Dad changed Addison's mind that day about who she was going to vote for in the election, but I'm certain she went to bed with more questions in her head than she had when she entered the student union that day. One thing our visit made obvious: the media had succeeded in making it uncool to be a conservative.

What, if anything, do their donors expect in return for their "investments"? We need to know this, because our country can't afford more trillion-dollar thank-you notes to campaign backers.

Sarah Palin

CHAPTER 20

Hey, Don't I Know You?

*Even now, after all that's happened in her life, she still has
time to stop and talk with the people she's come to know and
love, many of them friends from childhood.*
CHUCK HEATH SR.

O ur life as a family has been marked by adventure. We've
spent most of our lives enjoying the outdoors through
hunting, fishing, camping, hiking, and organized sports. That
lifestyle sometimes lends itself to a sense of self-sufficiency and
the false assurance that one can make it without the help of others. Quite to the contrary, my life, and the life of our family in
Alaska, has been spurred along, assisted, and made possible by the
help of friends. I've collected many things during my life, but of
all the things I've gathered around me, friends are one of the best.

Sally and I brought our family to Alaska sight unseen. Neither
she nor I had been there before, not even for a visit. Yet, in many
respects, it seemed as though Alaska was waiting for us as much as
we were waiting for it. Although the state was new territory for us
and we were on an uncharted personal journey, I found familiar
faces around every corner and in some of the most unlikely places.

As I mentioned earlier, when we were living in Skagway and
wanted to relocate to Anchorage, I stumbled across Russ Kramer,

an old friend from Sandpoint, Idaho. He was in a bar in Skagway. I heard his voice over the din of the crowd and found him sitting a few stools away. A phone call from him that night paved the way for the move that eventually brought us to Wasilla.

My father-in-law, Clem Sheeran, had a house in Richland, Washington, that sat atop a hill directly across the street from the public swimming pool. From the time the pool opened in the spring until it closed in the fall, his children pretty much lived over there in the water. They swam like fish until almost dark, then trudged across the street for dinner and collapsed in front of the television.

One summer evening, just before dark, Clem's youngest son, Mike, was watching television in the den and recovering from another day at the pool when the front doorbell rang. Reluctantly, he rolled off the sofa and lumbered through the house to see what poor slob was interrupting his favorite show. You can imagine his surprise when he opened the door and found a police officer standing on the front steps.

"Is that your green Rambler?" the officer asked, gesturing over his shoulder.

Mike's mouth fell open as he looked past the policeman to see the family's green Rambler sitting across the street...in the shallow end of the swimming pool.

As they soon discovered, Clem had driven home from work that afternoon, parked the car in the driveway, and failed to set the brake. While the family ate dinner and relaxed in front of the television, the car slowly rolled down the driveway, bounced across the street, crashed through the fence, and plunged into the pool. Thankfully, no one was injured.

I had heard that story a hundred times. It was repeated at family gatherings and retold almost every time someone remembered

Clem. I had no doubt the car rolled across the street to the pool but over the years I wondered just how much of it actually landed in the pool and how much of the story had been embellished by time.

A few years ago, while on a hunting trip near Cantwell, we went to dinner at a café just off the Denali Highway. Cantwell is a community of no real size about halfway between Anchorage and Fairbanks. It's located not far from the Denali Wilderness area, way out in the middle of nowhere. While we were sitting in the café, I heard a guy sitting near us mention that he had come to Alaska from the state of Washington. We got to talking, and he said he was from Richland. That was intriguing—a guy from Richland, Washington, way out in the Alaska bush sitting next to me, a man whose in-laws came from Richland—so I asked him what kind of work he did there. I was intrigued by the possibility of such a coincidental meeting and wondering if he was really telling the truth about where he was from. When he told me he had been a policeman, I asked if he knew my in-laws, Clem and Helen Sheeran. He grinned and said he knew them well. Then, without prompting from me, he repeated the story about the car rolling down the driveway and plunging into the swimming pool. He had been the police officer who investigated the incident.

My friend Dave Johnston had a cabin north of Wasilla. When the kids were young we used to go up there in the winter for a visit. Dave's cabin sat on a hillside that overlooked a lake and afforded a wonderful view of Mount McKinley. Steps led down from the cabin to a dock, where Dave had built a sauna. Sarah used to stay down there for hours at a time, heating up in the sauna and then jumping through a hole in the lake ice to the cold water below.

Dave did many things to earn a living, but his real passion was mountain climbing. In 1967 he was part of a team that became the first to complete a winter climb to the summit of Mount McKinley. That might not sound like much of a feat to those of you who don't climb, but I know from experience that was quite an accomplishment. At 20,320 feet above sea level, Mount McKinley is the highest peak in North America. But measured from base to peak it is the tallest mountain in the world. Few climbers have made it to the top and even fewer have done it in winter. Dave did it twice as a young man and later took his son, Galen, who was then only eleven years old. He's still the youngest person to make it to the top.

One of the men who went with Dave on the 1967 Mount McKinley trip was a guy named Ray Genet. In the late 1970s, Ray was part of an expedition that climbed Mount Everest. Ray's wife, Kathy, and his young son, Taras, then less than two years old, accompanied him for part of that climb. Taras became the youngest person to reach the Everest base camp.

After graduating from college, Chuck Jr. became a teacher. One of his first jobs took him to a school in Talkeetna, a small town about a hundred miles north of Anchorage and the traditional starting point for Mount McKinley expeditions. Taras Genet was a student in Chuck Jr.'s third-grade class. In spite of Alaska's enormous size, we keep bumping into each other.

We've met friends from the past in strange places, but we've made new ones, too. Many of those new friends showed up in our lives at strategic moments, sometimes with help that allowed us to achieve goals and dreams that would have been unattainable without their assistance. A few we met for the first time in dire circumstances. One of those friends was a man we called Bones.

Bones's real name was Gerry Groff. He lived at a camp out in the bush where he had spent his younger years mining, hunting, and trapping. We met him one rainy, cold night while caribou hunting.

Chuck Jr. and I had been in the woods several days when a storm blew over our tent. Wet and cold, we were in danger of becoming hypothermic and needed to get warm quickly. Chuck Jr. knew of a cabin about a mile from our location. He'd seen it on an earlier trip and thought it was abandoned. I wasn't sure we could make it that far but we had no other options, so we started in that direction.

After an hour's trek through the bush, we came to the cabin. Smoke curling from the flue told us it was occupied. Later we learned that Bones had been living there for years, though it was easy to see from the condition of the place why Chuck Jr. thought it was empty. Bones was suspicious of us and didn't want to let us inside, but after we explained our circumstances he allowed us to sleep in one of the outbuildings. We were grateful to have shelter from the weather and made ourselves comfortable for the night. The next morning, we ate breakfast with Bones. Over hot coffee and scrambled eggs, the three of us struck up a friendship that lasted many years.

Bones wasn't a young man when we stumbled upon him that night, but he was still active. In the winter he stayed near the cabin, occasionally hunting to keep himself supplied with meat. Through most of the summer months he mined for gold. Sally has several pieces of jewelry he made for her. He gave a few to Sarah, too. She wore them during the 2008 campaign.

Over the years, I noticed Bones was slowing down. Each year he spent less time outside, even in the warm months. Most winters, he only went as far as the outhouse. We helped him sign up for Social Security payments and after that he stopped hunting altogether. During the first few years that we knew him, we went out to his cabin and took him to town to buy supplies. Later, as he grew older, we bought the items for him and carried them out to the cabin. He didn't want much and we knew the list from memory.

A few months ago, Track and I took him a load of supplies. When we arrived we found the chimney for his stove was blocked and the interior of the cabin was covered with black soot. Bones's face was blackened, too. The things we'd brought him from a previous trip were still stacked in the corner, untouched. Outside, the ground was covered with snow, but there were no tracks leading to the outhouse.

We unplugged the flue for the stove and cleaned up the cabin. Then we helped clean up Bones also. By the time we left, I could see a little spark in his eyes but I knew he was in bad shape. Three or four days after we returned home, the telephone rang in our kitchen. A trapper called to say he'd found Bones dead in his cabin. Later that year, some of us gathered at his cabin and spread his ashes in the wilderness he knew and loved. He'd been a great friend who rescued us on a stormy night, helped us learn the art of mining, and embraced us with the warmth of friendship.

Not too long ago, Chuck Jr. was driving with his son near Livengood, an Alaska community about seventy miles north of Fairbanks. It was a thriving place during the gold-rush days but now only about thirty people live there. Somewhere along the way Chuck Jr. stopped to explore the banks of a creek and found a substantial quantity of gold. Two weeks later, he and I returned to assess the area more extensively. We both were interested in mining, and Chuck Jr. thought this would be a good place to set up a bigger operation. I was skeptical about the location. It was too good a location to have been missed and I was sure someone else had already filed a claim for it.

We set up a sluice box and I began shoveling dirt into it. Not long after that, a man appeared on the bank above me. He was shouting and cussing and wanted to know why I was there. I smarted off to him and he started down the bank toward me. I could see he had a pistol strapped to his hip, and I knew we were in for trouble.

When he came within a few feet of me he shouted again, "What the hell are you doing here?"

"Mining for gold," I replied, as calmly as I could.

"This is a private claim."

By then I recognized him and replied quietly, "Well, maybe I don't care." He put his hand on his pistol but before he could say anything else I continued, "Does the name Heath mean anything to you?"

He leaned back and glared at me. "I ought to shoot you right now, you old son of a bitch." He was Sam Eaves, one of my sixth-grade students from Chugiak. Years earlier, he'd been in one of those classes where we dissected moose entrails and rabbit eyes.

Sam came down to the sluice box and we renewed our acquaintance, remembered stories from the past, and caught each other up on the events of our lives. The years that separated us back when he was a student didn't seem so important then, and we were like old friends finding each other after a long absence. We've been back up there every year since and though we still miss Bones, Sam's a good friend too.

I've been bailed out of trouble many times in my life, most of the time by friends my own age. But in the spring of 1982, as the date for the Boston Marathon approached, the girls on the track team, all of them young enough to be my children, helped us with the gift of airline tickets for the trip. Without them, I would have been sitting at home reading the results of the race in the newspaper rather than running in it. But they weren't the only ones who came to our rescue.

The night before we left on the trip, Sally and I packed our clothes and things in a suitcase. We made sure we included jackets for the cool evening, running shorts and shoes for the marathon, and comfortable walking shoes for sightseeing afterward. All of those items were washed, dried, and placed carefully in the suitcase along with toiletries and all the things one carries for a trip. The next morning we loaded the suitcase into the car, checked one more time to make certain we had the airline tickets, then started from the house on the hour-long trip to the airport in Anchorage.

When we arrived at the airport ticket counter to check in for our flight, we realized the money for the trip—money we'd planned to spend on hotel, food, and sightseeing—was lying on the dresser at our home back in Wasilla. Our hearts sank. We'd arrived early enough to allow plenty of time to check our luggage and locate the proper departure gate, but driving back to the house and returning again to the airport was a two-hour trip. There wasn't enough time to do that and get back before the plane departed. If we were going to Boston, we had to keep moving. Otherwise, we would miss the race.

As I stood there, frustrated with myself for forgetting such an important thing, I glanced down the concourse and saw a group of passengers coming toward me. Among them was a friend who was just returning from a trip. The plane had parked at a gate down the concourse and he was walking up to the baggage area to claim his luggage. We greeted each other and when I explained our predicament, he reached into his pocket and took out a wad of cash. It was money left over from his trip. He pressed it into the palm of my hand and wished me well.

Sally and Chuck Sr. worked for nineteen years as wildlife specialists for the Department of Agriculture.

Sarah and Todd pick their net of red salmon in Bristol Bay.

Todd and Sarah viewing brown bears in the McNeil River in 2009.

The Heath and Palin families, 2010.

Sarah and her dad caribou hunting in the Arctic.

Chuck Sr. and Chuck Jr. in Valdez, 2010.

Sarah happily points to the results of her second win as mayor of Wasilla.

Chuck Jr. and Sally march proudly for Sarah in the July 4, 2006, parade.

The Heath and Palin clans at the Governor's Christmas Party, 2007.

The new governor of Alaska poses with her sisters, Heather and Molly, and brother, Chuck Jr., on election night 2006.

Sarah, Todd, and Piper at the finish line of the 2009 Iron Dog snowmachine race.

Proud dad Todd Palin with son Track at the basic training graduation ceremony, Fort Benning, Georgia.

Sarah and Piper cross Alfred Creek on the way to a gold claim.

The Palins, 2006: Willow, Bristol, Great-Grandma Lena, Grandma Blanche (Todd's mom), Sarah, Piper, and Todd.

Chuck Sr. and Sally on the campaign trail, 2008.

Sarah and her mom.

After Sarah's first major speech for the McCain-Palin campaign.

Sarah with her proud parents on the campaign trail, 2008.

Encouraged by his response, I moved down to the next gate. Another plane had just come to a stop on the ramp outside. Moments later, passengers appeared as they came from the jetway. I eagerly scanned the crowd and soon another familiar face appeared. Once again I explained my situation and again a friend loaned me cash left over from his trip. For the next hour and a half I repeated that process, meeting every plane that arrived at the airport. By the time we boarded our flight for Boston, I had $650 in my pocket, all of it borrowed from my friends, who were glad to help.

In 1964, my final year at Sandpoint, I taught ninth grade. I shared with my class the adventure we were embarking upon and the dream I had of finding a place where I could hunt and fish all year, and of actually living the outdoor life many of us imagined. They were a lively bunch of kids and it was a little sad to leave them. I coached the junior high teams and when I began I was looking forward to seeing them grow up. I needn't have worried about being around to see what they would become. Ten of them were captured by the dream I shared and now live within thirty minutes of me. Back then, when they were in the ninth grade, the ten-year age difference seemed like a wide gulf. Now, there's hardly any difference at all. We hunt, fish, and mine gold together. I'm a collector, and so are they. They also love to tell stories and when we're together our conversations often become a friendly game of "top that one" as we do our best to tell one more story better than the last.

That's the kind of life we introduced to our children. A life where no one is a stranger and everyone is a potential friend. I've heard others describe me as a tough guy. In my own mind I never thought of myself as tough. The few times I've allowed myself the introspection to address the matter, I've thought of myself as a friend. That's how I want to be known. And that's how I want my children to be known. We raised them to be friends and to never forget where they came from.

During the 2008 campaign, Sarah traveled to Cape Girardeau, Missouri, for a rally. The event was scheduled for the Show Me Center, a multiuse facility on the campus of Southeast Missouri State University. Todd Smith, son of Reid Smith, one of Sarah's coaches from her high school days, lived in the area. When Todd Smith found out Sarah was coming, he contacted Todd Palin to see if they could get a moment to say hello. He was glad to hear from them and made arrangements for them to get into the event. The two Todds had been great friends in high school. When the Smiths arrived at the Show Me Center, they found a long line of people waiting to get inside. They walked past the crowd and made their way up to the entrance. A campaign aide met them there and led them through the building to seats from which they could watch Sarah as she spoke. Afterward, someone from the campaign took them backstage to a green room where Sarah was greeting people. As they made their way down a crowded hallway, they passed another long line of people waiting to see Sarah. In that line were some of Rush Limbaugh's relatives, several of whom had been appointed to federal judgeships under previous Republican presidents and all of whom had been heavily involved in the state Republican Party. As the Smiths went by, someone muttered, "Who the hell are the Smiths?" To the many people gathered there that day, the Smiths were unimportant. To Sarah, they were friends, the most important people in the world.

Sarah has the gift of easily making friends and of never forgetting the ones she's always known. Even now, after all that's happened in her life, she still has time to stop and talk with the people she's come to know and love, many of them friends from childhood. In spite of serving as governor, campaigning with John McCain, and the notoriety she's gained since, she's still Sarah to those who know her. Accessibility has changed a little— she can't wander the aisles of Target or the grocery store the way she would have before, and she's frequently away from home—but friends always have been important to her and she still finds time to keep up with their lives. As Melanie Messenger said, "Sarah is a neighbor. She's just a person who lives here." Reid Smith added, "Sarah and her family are just like one of us." In a small town like Wasilla, that's the greatest compliment anyone could give. Christy Ridenour saw the same thing in her. "She's a politician normal people can relate to."

When Sarah's first book, *Going Rogue*, was released, the publisher sent her on a bus tour to promote it. The trip took her to the nation's major metropolitan areas, where she did interviews with local reporters and conducted book signings. While in the northern Virginia area, she did a book signing at a store in Roanoke. At that event we met O. P. Ditch, a retired veteran from the US Air Force. He had worked hard developing a website called Veterans for Sarah through which he solicited the support of others with prior military service in an effort to encourage Sarah to seek elected office. O. P. and his wife were among several attendees at the book signing selected to greet Sarah as she arrived at the store. They shook hands with her and had a moment to talk. He recalled, "When she talked to you, she looked you right in the eye and actually listened. It almost looked like it went right to her heart." She *did* take those conversations to heart and listened intently to hear what people had to say.

In November, we all spent Thanksgiving weekend in Richland, Washington, the town where Sally grew up and where her parents, Clem and Helen, had lived. While we were there, Sarah did a book signing at Hastings Bookstore. People camped out at the store for two days prior to the event just to see Sarah and have their book signed. Some of those standing in line told us they had driven as much as ten hours to get there. Later that weekend, Sarah and her cousin Greg Jones ran in a fun run. Thousands turned out for it, hoping to catch a glimpse of Sarah and making it the largest fun-run crowd ever.

On Thanksgiving Day, we gathered at Greg's house for dinner. His wife, Brandi, was a great hostess and did a fine job entertaining the group. Seventy people attended. Most of them were family members, but a few friends were invited too. Sometime that afternoon, the doorbell rang and one of us answered it. A woman outside identified herself and said she was a friend of Greg and Brandi and had been invited to dinner. She came inside and was walking through the house, looking for Sarah, when she ran into Greg. Again she introduced herself and said she was a friend of Greg and Brandi. As you might expect, Greg didn't know her and was ready to show her to the door, but Sarah overheard them talking and intervened. She met with the woman and spent a few minutes talking to her.

While we ate, reporters and cameramen were waiting outside. Sarah wanted to invite them inside too, but Sally's sisters objected. The day had been disrupted enough already and they didn't want pictures of their Thanksgiving dinner in the newspapers. Sarah wouldn't have minded one bit. She's been like that most of her life.

One of the people who accompanied Sarah on the book tour was Juanita Fuller, a longtime friend facing the challenges of a hectic life. Sarah knew Juanita needed a break and invited her to join the tour as a way of helping her get a fresh perspective on life. No one asked Sarah to do that, she just knew Juanita needed her support, as Juanita had supported her in the past. Sarah always has been like that. She might not see her friends every day, but she's never more than a phone call away and ready to lend a hand at a moment's notice.

That ability to connect with people is one of the reasons she's been successful in politics. She has an uncanny way of remembering names and a penchant for conveying a sense of genuine interest in the lives of the people she meets. Even casual acquaintances, sometimes people she's met only once, seem locked forever in her mind. That ability helps her project a sense of authentic concern and conveys a level of comfort that makes her appear approachable.

Crowds of strangers in places far from Alaska feel as if she's one of them. They respond physically by pressing close for a chance to touch her hand or catch her eye. Every day they send her packages containing family photo albums and pieces of artwork. One supporter sent a display of medals he received from military service. Bobby Hooper, a retiree from Georgia, sent her several hand-carved wooden writing pens. He saw her as someone who was "just trying to do the right thing for the country" and wanted to show his appreciation.

That sense of "approachableness" helped Sarah connect with voters and propelled her to the heights of political success. I like to think she picked that up from us and from growing up in Alaska.

And I can tell you from experience that sudden and relentless reform never sits well with entrenched interests and power brokers.

Sarah Palin

CHAPTER 21

The Election

They shouted and screamed as Sarah arrived. She took the
stage and gave her last speech of the campaign. And once
again, the crowd gave an enthusiastic response. I still
get goose bumps thinking about it.
CHUCK HEATH JR.

As the weeks went by, the 2008 campaign picked up even greater momentum. Sarah's already-full schedule became more crowded than ever as she raced at breakneck speed, criss-crossing the country in a headlong dash toward Election Day. Some weeks she did as many as five rallies per day, which was exhausting not just for her but for everyone involved. The rallies I attended with her left me drained, and I could only imagine what it was like to do them back-to-back and day after day.

Although she was tired, she seemed to use the crowds' energy to keep herself going. Her mind was sharp and clear but her body showed signs of the stress she endured. At the beginning of the campaign she already was slender but as the days went by I could see she was losing weight. Through those final weeks of the campaign, I met her at several events and when I gave her a hug I could tell she was even smaller than before. Every ounce of energy she possessed was focused on pushing through to the end of the campaign. Like a marathoner on the last portion of the race, she was fighting through a wall of fatigue to reach the finish line. She was tough, but the pace she maintained during the run-up to the election was amazing.

The day before the election I was in Nevada, working from the campaign office in Reno. With Election Day only hours away, our work was coming to a close. Sarah's final campaign events were set for Nevada, but almost every hour of the day leading up to those events was filled with activity as she made her way into the state. By the time she arrived in Nevada, she'd appeared in nonstop rallies through Iowa, Ohio, Missouri, and Colorado.

Events in Nevada began with a stop in Reno. Mom, Dad, and I met her that afternoon at the airport and rode with her to the Reno-Sparks Livestock Events Center. Todd's parents were with us too. Sarah was tired, but once again the energy of the crowd refreshed her. She came alive as she stepped onto the stage and delivered a rousing speech. At the end, Dad whispered that he wanted to say something from the podium. Sarah handed him the microphone and he said, "Years ago, I taught Sarah how to field dress a moose. Tomorrow, I'm going to teach her how to field dress a donkey!" It was the kind of corny remark we'd heard all our life, and not just from Dad but from many of our friends and acquaintances in Alaska. Todd cringed. The crowd went wild.

From there we worked our way to Elko, Nevada, a mining town not unlike many we'd seen back home. We arrived at the high school a little after eleven that night and slightly behind schedule. Even though the hour was late, the gym was filled with more than three thousand raucous supporters. They shouted and screamed as Sarah entered the building. She took a moment to greet them, shaking hands with those nearby, then stepped to the stage for her last speech of the campaign. Once again, the crowd gave an enthusiastic response, yelling, clapping, and stomping their feet. I still get goose bumps thinking about it—the crowd, their enthusiasm, and the realization that we were at the end of a physically taxing two months.

When the rally ended, we boarded a bus with the campaign staff and headed to a hotel. Sarah and Todd went to the airport for a flight back to Alaska so they could vote at home. The next morning they cast their vote at the City Hall in Wasilla, then left immediately for a return flight. They rejoined us in Phoenix, Arizona, as we gathered at the Biltmore Hotel for the campaign's official election-night watch party.

Those of us who had remained overnight in Nevada arrived in Phoenix early on Election Day. Mom and Dad were with us, as were several of Mom's sisters and cousins. I located my room, deposited my luggage on the bed, and walked over to the reception hall. The campaign staff was gathered there awaiting election results. The mood in the room was understandably tense. McCain's staff had been working for the past two years to reach that day. In the months since the convention we joined them in pouring our bodies and souls into the election effort. Yet events in the fall of 2008 seemed to conspire against us as the economy dropped into a free-fall and financial markets spiraled out of control. I wasn't sure we could weather the perfect political storm that faced us.

With the difference in time zones—Arizona was on Mountain Standard Time—election results would begin trickling in from states in the east by late afternoon, a few hours away. I wandered around the room, talking to friends and looking for ways to pass the time. Minutes seemed to tick by slowly as we waited for the numbers to arrive.

Exit polls showed the election tipping Obama's way, but when

I asked campaign insiders about it they told me not to pay attention to the early results. They assured me that those preliminary indicators were often incorrect. I was cautiously optimistic and did my best to remain upbeat, but what I saw from those voting samples and my own intuition left me uneasy.

About four in the afternoon, actual results arrived as polls closed in states along the Atlantic seaboard. We won in Tennessee, Kentucky, and South Carolina. Barack Obama won Connecticut, Delaware, Maine, Maryland, Massachusetts, and several more to take an early lead in the electoral votes. An hour later, he picked up Wisconsin, Minnesota, Michigan, New York, and Pennsylvania. We added the Republican strongholds of Alabama and Georgia. The electoral count stood at 174 for Obama and 64 for McCain.

Results continued to appear as polls closed in a steadily rolling wave that swept across the nation. As tallies from each of the remaining states were reported, the mood in the room at the Biltmore went from tense to dour. I did my best to keep up the optimistic rhetoric, right to the end, but I had suspected from earlier in the day that the election was not going to end the way we'd hoped. That evening, I watched as those suspicions became reality.

By nine that night, an Obama victory was obvious. Most of the news broadcasts projected him as the winner, a fact confirmed by our own internal campaign reports. Images from the park in Chicago, where a crowd of his supporters had been gathering, showed us what we already knew. They would be the ones celebrating that night.

A few minutes later, aides from the campaign rounded us up and led us toward a stage that had been constructed on the hotel lawn. When we were all in place, John and Cindy McCain emerged, followed by Sarah and Todd. After a warm welcome from the crowd, John stepped up to the podium and delivered the concession speech. "My friends," he began, "we have come to the end of a long journey. The American people have spoken, and they have spoken clearly." He praised Barack Obama for breaking the color barrier, for his convincing job in delivering a vision of hope for America, and wished him well during his term in office. He thanked Sarah for being a great campaigner, acknowledged her as a new voice in the party, and thanked our family for enduring a rough-and-tumble presidential campaign. Then he ended with a final plea for unity. "Tonight, more than any night, I hold in my heart nothing but love for this country and for all its citizens. Whether they supported me or Senator Obama, I wish Godspeed to the man who was my former opponent and will be my president." It was a good speech, delivered in typical McCain style—slightly awkward, a little brusque, and straight from the heart.

Though disappointed with the election result, the crowd rallied for one more round of cheers and applause. Like all of us, they had hoped for a victory but, having been denied that, their response left little doubt which candidate they supported.

As music began to play, John and Cindy lingered on the stage with Sarah and Todd, posing for pictures and waving to the crowd. Then, with a final handshake, the four of them filed down the steps into the sea of supporters. As she passed by me, Sarah said quietly, "Darn it! I had a great speech I wanted to give to thank McCain and all of our supporters who worked so hard on this campaign." I found out later that McCain staff members had intervened to prevent her from giving her own speech.

As the crowd drifted away and the final official campaign event drew to a close, our family gathered in Sarah's hotel room, where we had an impromptu family-and-friends party. The mood was surprisingly upbeat considering the defeat we'd just experienced. Everyone had worked as hard as possible on the campaign and, though we all wanted a different outcome, we found solace in the fact that we'd given our all to the effort. We also realized that Sarah was going to emerge from the election, in spite of the defeat, as a new voice in the Republican Party and one many would consider as a potential candidate in 2012. Sarah seemed happier and more relaxed than she'd been in months.

The following morning, we had breakfast in a restaurant at the Biltmore. As I was walking to our table I noticed Jon Voight, the actor, seated across the way. We had met at the Republican Convention and struck up a friendship. He waved me over to his table and asked me to join him. I sat with him a few minutes that morning, talking about the election over a cup of coffee. As I was about to leave, he told me to give Sarah his best and to tell her that her job wasn't done. I wasn't sure what he meant by that, but I told him I would pass the message to her.

After breakfast, we all joined Sarah and Todd at the pool. The Arizona sunshine was quite different from the weather that awaited us in Alaska. After an hour or two, we returned to the room, gathered our bags, and rode in our last campaign motorcade from the hotel to the Phoenix airport. There, we boarded a jet and flew toward home.

In Anchorage, a large contingent of supporters awaited us as the plane taxied to a stop in front of the hangar where we'd first departed for this adventure eight weeks earlier. As we came down the steps from the plane they called to us, shouting and waving McCain-Palin signs as if the election were still in doubt. For a moment, it seemed like just another stop on the endless circuit of rallies and events that had been our lives through the previous two months. And then I realized it was just us and the crowd. The aides and Secret Service agents, who had been so obviously present throughout the campaign, were no longer with us. We were on our own. Or so it seemed.

Across the continent in North Carolina, Karen Allen had been watching election-night events on the television in her living room. As we stood on the stage at the Biltmore, listening to John McCain deliver the concession speech, Karen listened too. The words McCain said that night landed with a thud in her soul. The look on Sarah's face, however, stirred her to action. "No!" she remembered shouting to herself. "This is not the way this is going to end."

As we flew toward Alaska to pick up our lives, Karen rose from the sofa and went to work on the future. She contacted friends and family who shared her view that the fight over the issues Sarah raised in the campaign must continue. Gradually, a plan developed and their initial ad-hoc group became Organize for Palin, a nationwide, grassroots organization. Focused on the issues Sarah championed—the sanctity of life, strong national defense, integrity in government, and an end to crony capitalism, among others—they vowed to continue the fight to transform America. Karen explained it: "Before Sarah came along, I kept my political views to myself and didn't tell anyone my opinions. But not anymore. She empowered a movement."

In a matter of months, Organize for Palin had coordinators working in thirty-eight states. "Palin supporters are amazing people," Karen commented. "They will volunteer to do anything that supports her values." They participated in conservative political events and rallied their members to attend Sarah's speeches, book signings, and other appearances. Asked about that sense of connection between Sarah and her supporters, Karen said, "People who support Sarah see themselves in her." Though we didn't realize it at the time, others were equally energized by Sarah's presence in the campaign, some of them from the moment Sarah stepped onto the national stage.

In Minnesota, Debbie Turner stood in her kitchen, preparing dinner for her family and listening to Sarah's convention acceptance speech. The words resonated deep inside her. Debbie grew up in California as the daughter of staunchly Republican parents. "My father was a Ronald Reagan fan before he [Reagan] ever ran for office." While still in school, Debbie worked in television and appeared in numerous commercials. In 1965, she won the role of Marta von Trapp in the feature film *The Sound of Music*. As she listened to Sarah, she was struck by both the ideas of the speech and the delivery. Debbie recalled, "I remember thinking, 'Who is this woman? She sounds like Ronald Reagan.' She had the same effect on me as when I used to listen to him."

When *Going Rogue* was released, Debbie purchased a copy. Just a few chapters into it she read where Sarah described how much she'd enjoyed *The Sound of Music* as a child. As kids, she and our sisters really loved that film. They watched it with our mother over and over, then they sang the songs at the top of their voices.

After reading about Sarah's fascination with the film, Debbie purchased multiple copies of the book and started looking for a way to get them autographed. Not long after that, Sarah did a book signing at the Mall of America in Bloomington, Minnesota, thirty minutes from Debbie's home. On the day of the signing, Debbie took her daughters, Brooke, Angela, and Kate, and headed out to the mall, arriving a little after four in the morning. "I told my daughters that by getting there that early we would be sure to be at the front of the line. When we arrived, there were a thousand people already waiting at the store." They stood in line for seven hours. "I've never stood in line for anything, but I stood in line to meet Sarah Palin."

When Debbie finally reached the table, Sarah was undone. "You have no idea how much I loved that movie," she said, beaming. "I am starstruck to see you." Our mother was equally enamored of the film, and when she met Debbie, the two quickly became friends. A few months later, Debbie and Angela traveled to Alaska with a friend, Jacquie Emmer, and visited in our parents' home. Debbie even made a brief appearance in a video Sarah created promoting the involvement of women in politics.

In the months following the 2008 election, we learned of many more people across the nation who had been awakened to a new sense of political duty and a fresh call to political action. Many of them would make the trek to Alaska, drive hundreds of miles to book signings and political events, and wait for hours to see Sarah, to let her know they still cared, and to assure her that she was not alone. With their help, we would all come to see the meaning of what Jon Voight had told me in the restaurant before we left Phoenix—the job is not yet done. But that night, when we arrived back in Anchorage after the election and the gathering in Arizona, it seemed as though we were left to fend for ourselves.

Now it is time for us to go our way, neither bitter nor vanquished, but instead confident in the knowledge that there will be another day, and we may gather once more, and find new strength, and rise to fight again.

Sarah Palin

CHAPTER 22

What's Next?

Many people ask me about Sarah's future and whether she will run for office again. To be honest, I don't know.
CHUCK HEATH SR.

When the 2008 presidential campaign ended, we all thought we could return to Alaska and pick up our lives where we left off, with little disruption to what had been our normal routine. For Sally and me, that was more or less true. Sally's week fell into the usual pattern of church, Bible study, and life with our friends. I went back to hunting, fishing, and rambling around the yard with Bo, our dog. For Sarah and Todd, however, life was anything but routine.

As the weeks went by, the press, which had been ruthless during the campaign, continued to hound Sarah and her family. If she spoke out, they did their best to make her look ignorant and out of touch. If she kept quiet, they painted her as wounded, cowering, and in retreat. When she countered the accusations they continued to make, they accused her of being petty and wearing her feelings on her sleeve. All the while the ethics complaints continued to mount and with them the legal expense of defending them. Very quickly, governing from the governor's office ground to a halt as more and more time was devoted to collecting information necessary to respond to the complaints. With bipartisanship destroyed in the legislature, efforts to move her agenda forward went nowhere.

An ancient philosopher named Sun Tzu once said the person who chooses the location of the battle determines the outcome. As Sarah looked at her situation, she realized her opposition was forcing her to play by their rules and the state of Alaska was paying the price for it through a governor's office now rendered largely ineffective. To change the outcome, she had to change the battlefield. As she considered her options, she turned to the notion of resigning.

Discussion of that option was tightly held. I didn't know about it until afterward. As we have said elsewhere in this book, we found out she was going to resign when she made a public announcement. Sarah, Todd, Meghan Stapleton, and Kris Perry knew about it long before as they discussed the ramifications of that potential decision.

"Many people thought she resigned to get a book deal," Meghan recalled. "We already had the book deal. But I had to tell her, 'If you do this. If you resign, the publisher may withdraw that deal. You won't be governor, and you won't be a candidate and they could say, "We don't want to do it." You could lose everything.'"

Sarah replied, "If it costs me everything, then that's the way it will be." She was determined to return the governor's office to executing its constitutional responsibilities, even if that decision had devastating personal consequences for her. As Meghan observed, "She didn't have speaking engagements and we weren't sure she'd have a book deal when it was over."

The announcement surprised me, but when Sarah explained her reasons I understood what she was doing. The goal of her political career never had been to promote herself, but to do what was right for Alaska. Self-sacrificing politicians are few and far between and when one comes along, we often find it hard to believe they actually would make decisions that are in the best interest of the citizens, even if those decisions are to the politicians' detriment. We ask for that kind of leadership and when we get it we find it difficult to accept. Sarah was one of those rare politicians who chose the good of the people over her own best interests.

Following her resignation, the publishing company held to their book deal and Sarah focused on finishing her first manuscript. She also received invitations to a number of public appearances around the country. Some of them were speaking engagements at political and corporate gatherings. Others were less politically driven. As much as possible, she included members of her extended family in those events, though not all of us at the same time.

Chuck Jr. accompanied Sarah when she appeared on *The Tonight Show with Jay Leno*. Several months later, Molly went with her to New York for a gala honoring *Time* magazine's "100 Most Influential People in the World." While filming episodes for the television show *Sarah Palin's Alaska*, we flew with Sarah and a camera crew up to a camp on the Kavik River near Prudhoe Bay. The camp was operated by a woman named Sue Aikens, who came to Alaska as a child, fell in love with the wilderness, and was never comfortable anywhere else.

In November 2009, when Sarah launched a tour to promote the release of *Going Rogue*, Sally was part of the traveling group. Sarah invited me to come too, but I declined, preferring the anonymity of Wasilla to life on the road. A few days into the tour, Sally called me and said, "You need to get out here. We're having a blast." So, I picked up Sarah's daughter Piper, and we flew east together to join them. I'm glad we did.

Seeing the reaction of the people who turned out at those book events helped me get past much of the frustration I'd felt over the way Sarah had been treated during the 2008 campaign. People came to the events in droves and stood in line for hours just to get a glimpse of her. They cheered when she arrived and when they finally made it up to the table where she was signing books, they cried and gasped and stood in awe. I was amazed that she could evoke such a reaction and was heartened by the response. I'd carried some personal angst since the 2008 campaign. Not really anger, not really bitterness, just the sense that she'd been wronged. Seeing the response to her on the book tour helped me get past all that. The tour also included a side trip that proved to be one of the greatest delights of our lives—an overnight stay in Montreat, North Carolina.

In 2006, a fire swept through the coastal village of Hooper Bay, wiping out homes and stores and leaving many families in ruin. Franklin Graham, who has a summer cabin in Alaska, heard about the devastation. He brought his Samaritan's Purse organization to Hooper Bay and helped rebuild some of the homes. Then in 2009, before she resigned, Sarah and Franklin worked together to deliver relief to families living in and around Marshall and Russian Mission, communities in the interior of Alaska that were hard-hit by winter weather and the economic downturn. They flew food packages to the villages and joined in handing them out to needy families. While on that trip, Franklin invited Sarah to meet with his father, Billy Graham.

Not long after I joined the *Going Rogue* book tour, Franklin followed through on that invitation. We left the bus caravan, flew by private jet to Asheville, North Carolina, then drove by car to

Dr. Graham's residence. Our group included Sarah, Piper, Trig, Sally and me, and Sally's sister Katie Johnson.

For us, this was one of the highlights of our lives. Sally and I had attended a Billy Graham evangelistic crusade when he came to Alaska in the 1970s, but we never imagined we'd actually get to meet him, much less visit him in his home. Later, Sally told me that while we were talking, she kept thinking of how her parents would have enjoyed being there with him. Although they were a dedicated Catholic family, Clem and Helen watched every broadcast of Billy Graham's crusades. Clem particularly enjoyed the music of George Beverly Shea. All I could think of was how glad I was that Sally was there. She had been enamored of Billy Graham's preaching all her life.

At the time we met with him, Dr. Graham was ninety-one years old. He may have slowed physically, but he was still sharp and alert. We sat with him around the fireplace in a lively and engaging conversation that seemed to last just a few minutes. Actually, we talked for two hours. Finally, and reluctantly, we excused ourselves and let him and Sarah have some time for a private conversation. A little while later, we were ushered into the dining room for a wonderful dinner. Afterward, we were led out to a comfortable guest cabin near the main house and settled in for some much-needed rest.

As we lay in bed that night I thought of how far we'd come—not just from Wasilla to Montreat, but the span of our lives. No one could have predicted things would turn out as they had and none of us had tried to shape events toward this particular end. We'd just focused on doing our best to live a life that meant something. We worked hard, gave each endeavor all we had to offer, and events took us from one adventure to the next.

Sarah had entered politics as a candidate for a seat on the

Wasilla City Council with the goal of making the town a better place to live. All she wanted was to make a difference. To live a life that counted. She campaigned diligently and won that first race decisively. Later she ran for mayor and served two terms. Wasilla is a small town. It was even smaller back then and everyone knew everyone else. When she first ran for office, people still dropped by the house for a visit without calling ahead to see if you were home. No one had an unlisted telephone number and if you didn't know where someone lived, the postman would tell you. Accessibility wasn't an issue.

As Sarah campaigned for statewide offices, first as a candidate for lieutenant governor and then governor, she became more widely known. Requests from reporters and the general public became more frequent. That greater notoriety allowed her to reach a larger audience and gave her a platform from which to address an expanding array of issues.

With the city council, the issues she faced were local—property tax, sales tax, garbage pickup, and the need for infrastructure improvements. Later, as mayor, she faced many of those same issues, along with the need for an adequate regional hospital, better roads, stronger local businesses, and better city services. She led the fight to accomplish those goals and in doing so had great success. Each success helped her see the larger possibilities that lay ahead. Like ever widening circles, her experiences took her further and further from the limitations many assigned to her as a graduate of little Wasilla High School and a resident of a small town. And with each step she moved further from the people she'd known and loved. She was still the same Sarah everyone had seen from childhood; she just wasn't as available as she'd once been.

The nastiness of the 2008 campaign made accessibility an even more important issue and drove home the dichotomy between the potential to make lasting public changes and the loss of personal privacy. While reporters ripped into Sarah, they tore into the rest of us too. Few private citizens understand the raw treatment behind the articles they read in the news media. Though we've found ways to get past most of the anger we felt during the 2008 campaign, those two issues—opportunity for public service and loss of personal privacy—remain a source of tension for Sarah, Todd, and our extended family.

Early in her term as governor, Sarah enjoyed bipartisan political support. Many of her accomplishments were gained with the help of Democrats in the state legislature. Her entry into the 2008 presidential election as John McCain's running mate changed that.

While she was governor, the issues she faced were state issues. Once she stepped onto the stage at the convention in St. Paul, she became a candidate for national office. In the ensuing campaign, national politics trumped state issues. Alaska Democrats who previously supported her were forced to take sides based on loyalty to the national party in the presidential election. Voting for state initiatives proposed by Sarah—a Republican and one now on the national ticket—became a question of party loyalty. With state elections approaching, Alaska's Democratic legislators were left vulnerable to attack from rivals within their own party if they supported her proposals and programs. As a result, bipartisan support evaporated.

Within the state Republican Party, some who held core leadership positions saw the 2008 campaign as an opportunity to neutralize Sarah's widespread popularity among Alaska voters. All they had to do was stand quietly by and watch while Democrats unleashed the dogs of war on her. And that's what happened.

For the public, the party geared up for the presidential campaign. It opened offices, printed bumper stickers, and distributed yard signs, but when Democratic researchers and their friends in the media descended on Alaska, many of those Republican leaders watched quietly as seasoned political operatives ripped into Sarah's character and reputation.

If I sound bitter, I'm not—not now. I'm just a father who was forced to watch while his daughter's character was disemboweled by people who claim to have our nation's best interest at heart. I think you can see now why I've been more interested in hunting, fishing, and sports than a life lived in the public arena.

Sarah, however, is not like me. She doesn't like the way she was treated, but she's not interested in retreating, either. Like Clem, her grandfather, Sarah is a fighter with a clear sense of moral certainty. For her, life has presented very few gray areas. Most of the time, she sees things only as right or wrong. Rarely has she confronted a situation with ambiguity. That sense of moral certainty has been one of her greatest strengths. It has also made her a lightning rod for criticism and attack from those who see the world through amoral eyes.

Many have mistaken her approach to life and politics as an assertion that she is somehow perfect or at least better than others. Nothing could be further from the truth. She's not perfect, and she would be the first to tell you that. She's not simple, either. Sarah is the most complex person I've ever known. Labels like conservative, patriotic, faithful, believer, and friend all apply to her, but they do not begin to adequately describe the depth of character she holds or define the response she makes to the range of issues that pique her interest.

Many people ask me about Sarah's future and whether she will run for office again. To be honest, I don't know, but I'll support her in whatever she does. She has talent and ability, and I want her to make the most of every opportunity that comes her way. We reared our children to think for themselves, and they've all done a great job making their own decisions. I would be proud of Sarah if she ran for office, and equally proud if she spent her time writing and speaking. She has a good mind, a kind heart, and a great spirit. Whatever she decides, I'm sure it will come as a surprise to all of us and then we'll be off on a new adventure.

ABOUT THE AUTHORS

CHUCK HEATH SR. is a retired science teacher and coach. He received a bachelor's degree from Eastern Washington University, and a master's of education degree from the University of Alaska, Anchorage. A former college football player, he transitioned to distance running later in life and became an accomplished marathoner, even representing Alaska in the Boston Marathon. Chuck has spent a half-century exploring the wilderness of Alaska while hunting, fishing, gold mining, hiking, and skiing. His two greatest accomplishments in life have been making the move from Idaho to Alaska and watching all four of his children graduate from college. Chuck and Sally, his wife of fifty-one years, live in Wasilla, Alaska.

CHUCK HEATH JR. followed in his father's footsteps and currently is a teacher and coach in Anchorage, Alaska. He received a bachelor of science degree from the University of Idaho, where he was a member of the Sigma Alpha Epsilon fraternity and the Vandals football team. When he's not in the classroom teaching, Chuck enjoys playing adult league hockey. Although he has hunted and fished his entire life, Chuck's passion for over twenty years has been gold mining. He lives in Anchorage with his wife, Abby, and his three children, Kier, Teko, and Sophia.